"There is no better 'how to' book to prepare us for success in the 21st century. With wisdom and clarity, Jo Condrill brilliantly shows the way and provides the tools!"
—Pauline Shirley, International President 1994-1995,
Toastmasters International

"This is the best primer I've seen since 'Dick and Jane'! Read it with your pen in hand. Discover things you never knew before and become reacquainted with things you have forgotten."
—Reba Eichelberger
Counselor and Attorney-at-Law

"Whether a rookie in life, or a seasoned veteran, we all need to take time to tune up our lives. Often, unfortunately, we allow external forces or events to choose when and where this happens. Jo Condrill, has made it easy for you to 'take charge' of this very important life step with this book. Get it. Read it. Apply it. Don't wait for something to happen! Make it happen! This book will help you. I promise."
—Jim Blasingame
The Small Business Advocate
smallbusinessadvocate.com

"Jo Condrill continues to enlighten her audience with insightful, common sense, 'how to's' that allow readers to focus toward achievement of their dreams through a step by step process."
—Pat Gransbury
First State Woman Editor
President, Sussex Business and Professional Women

"An inspiring call to action that would help all of us to dare to make our hopes and dreams real. The clear and easy-to-follow exercises are what make this book a stand out as a valuable personal development tool...an excellent guide to career planning for the young person at the threshold of their life or for the experienced professional yearning to make a change. I recommend that you add this powerful tool to your personal growth toolbox."
  –James A. Lippold, MSW, Executive Director,
  Lincoln County (WA) Counseling Center

"The positive message in this very practical 'how to' book gives anyone a way to find their direction or get it back. I read it at the perfect moment in my life to test the truth of what it offered. I highly recommend its timeless message."
  –Dolly Ogawa
  Managing Editor, Antelope Valley Journal

"Condrill's book is an inspiring prescription for the brave! In her Millennium Primer: TAKE CHARGE OF YOUR LIFE, Jo Condrill tells you how to catch that falling star."
  –Marylee King
  Director of Student Learning Services
  Marylhurst University

"Read this book and discuss it with a friend. If he or she did the same with yet another, a huge quiet (analog) momentum among us all would perpetuate on par with the electronic internet revolution sweeping our lives. Take this step to develop your vision; we all have one. Will you bring it to life for us?"
  –Charlotte M. Thornton
  Founder, 21st Century Design & Development/
  Universal Maglev

A Millennium Primer

By Jo Condrill and Bennie Bough, Ph.D.

*101 Ways to Improve Your
Communication Skills Instantly*

A Millennium Primer:
TAKE CHARGE OF YOUR LIFE

Jo Condrill

*Best Wishes,
Jo Condrill*

GoalMinds® Los Angeles, CA

A GoalMinds® Book
Copyright © 1999 by Jo Condrill

All rights reserved. No part of this book may be reproduced or transmitted in any form or by any means, electronic or mechanical, including photocopying, recording or by any information storage and retrieval system without written permission from the author, except for the inclusion of brief quotations in a review.

Published in the United States of America

from Vision to Victory

http://www.goalminds.com

Publisher's Cataloging-in-Publication Data
Condrill, Jo.
    A Millennium Primer : Take Charge of Your Life / Jo Condrill. -- 1st ed.
    p. cm.
    Includes bibliographical references and index.
    LCCN: 99-91315
    ISBN: 0-9661414-5-8

    1. Success—Psychological aspects.
2. Self-actualization (Psychology) I. Title.

BF637.S8C66 1999   158
                     QBI99-1511

Text design by Joe Arunski

Manufactured in the United States of America

First Edition 1999

10 9 8 7 6 5 4 3 2

Dedication

*This book is dedicated
in loving memory, to my father,
Freddie Founteno, who
always challenged me to be my best, and
to my mother, Ida Donatto Founteno,
with love and gratitude.*

Contents

Introduction   xvii

SECTION ONE: ENVISION YOUR FUTURE

Chapter 1 Dream Great Dreams   21

Chapter 2 Define Your terms   24
    Vision
    Dreams
    Mission
    Purpose
    Success

Chapter 3 Take Time to Think   26
    Do a Lifeline Exercise
    Review Your Life Story
    Look at Your Personal Rule Book
    Know What You Don't Want

Chapter 4 Use Your Creative Imagination   32
    Imagine
    Explore Possibilities
    Expand Your Thinking
    Have Fun

Chapter 5 Design Your Future   37
    Look at the Big Picture
    Find Time to Dream
    Stop Muddling Through
    Transform Your Dream
    Discover the Power
    Proceed with Caution

    YOUR TURN—TAKE ACTION   42

SECTION TWO: MAKE A CONSCIOUS DECISION

Chapter 6 Exercise Your Power to Choose   49
    Analyze the Dream You Selected
    Evaluate
    Make a Decision

Contents

Chapter 7 Reach for A Dream Catcher   53

Chapter 8 Evaluate the Dream   55
    What are the Risks?
    Look for Potential Obstacles
      and Solutions
    Explore Options
    Estimate the Costs
    Identify Resources
    Find the Benefits

Chapter 9 Practice "What If" Drills   61
    Ask Others
    Ask Yourself
    Weigh the Options
    Try It On

Chapter 10 Make a Commitment   66
    Look Inside
    Make a Conscious Decision
    Persevere

    YOUR TURN—TAKE ACTION   70

SECTION THREE: FORM A SUPPORT TEAM

Chapter 11 Share Your Vision   79
    Make a List
    First Look for Supportive People
    Break Bread with Them
    Let Them Help You
    Understand the Law of Reciprocity
    10 Ways to Show Appreciation
    Get Others Excited About Your Vision
    Continue to Build
    Keep in touch

Chapter 12 Tell It Like It Is   87
    Provide Solid Information
    Face the Fear
    Practice These Techniques
    Communicate Clearly

Contents

    Acknowledge Support and Involvement
    Let Them Know You Know the Challenges
    When You Face Ridicule
    Be Enthusiastic, Even Passionate About Your Vision

Chapter 13 Let Them Talk   93
    Pay Attention
    Become a More Effective Listener
    Make Them Feel Important

Chapter 14 Lessons Harry Taught Me   96

    10 Keys to Communicating Your Vision

    YOUR TURN—TAKE ACTION   99

SECTION FOUR: STRATEGIC ALLIANCES

Chapter 15 Forming a Strategic Alliance   105
    Study the Concept
    A Two-Person Alliance
    My Not So Secret Formula
    Alliance in Action

Chapter 16 Take the Initiative   111
    Why Form Such a Group?
    Know Whom to Select
    Lead the Group
    Form Ground Rules
    Decide on Meetings
    How Long Does a Group Stay Together?
    Set the Agenda
    Make the Tough Decisions
    Try It

Chapter 17 How an Effective Strategic Alliance
    Worked for Me   118

    Survey Responses

    YOUR TURN—TAKE ACTION   123

Contents

SECTION FIVE: PLAN AND IMPLEMENT

Chapter 18 Make It Happen   129
    Envision Your Desired Outcome
    Develop a Strategy

Chapter 19 Develop an Action Plan   132
    Make a List of Known Activities
    Develop Family Support
    Ask for Help
    Refine Your List
    Develop a Time Line
    Focus on Essentials

Chapter 20 Visualize Don't Fantasize   139
    Create a Goal Poster
    Find the Time
    Practice Positive Affirmations
    How This Worked for Me

Chapter 21 Implement the Plan   146
    Take the First Step
    Be Persistent
    Know When to Walk Away
    Develop a Sense of Urgency

Chapter 22 Lessons Learned During the   150
    Burial of the Unknown Soldier

    YOUR TURN—TAKE ACTION   153

SECTION SIX: MEASURE YOUR PROGRESS

Chapter 23 Keep Score   161
    The Human Computer
    Write It Down
    Establish a Base Line
    Know Where the Goal Line Is
    Decide What Victory Is
    Work with Others

Contents

Chapter 24 Take Care of Details   167
    State the Rules
    Conduct IPR's
    Provide Feedback

Chapter 25 How We Kept Score   171

    YOUR TURN—TAKE ACTION   173

SECTION SEVEN: REWARDS

Chapter 26 Reward Efforts   181
    Know When to Praise
    Give Something Appropriate
    Tie Rewards to Goal Getting

Chapter 27 Please the Recipient   184
    Know What to Praise
    Know How to Praise
    Give Them What They Want
    Think of Creative Ways to
      Reward People

Chapter 28 Reward Yourself   189

    Your Gold Medal of Life!   191

    YOUR TURN—TAKE ACTION   192

Selected Readings   195

Index   200

Acknowledgments

Many people have blessed me in many ways during the creation of this book. I am very grateful to them all. Marcia Williams was the first to brainstorm these ideas with me. Barbara and John Hunt, Sara Summers, and Hsu Terry Wang soon participated in a seminar to help shape the concepts. Many seminars followed with hundreds of people participating. Michael and Nancy Wardinski provided critical review and encouraging words. Bess Crouch, my sister, encouraged, assisted, and challenged me to be my best.

Donna Holley, David Neilson, Harry Truman, Wayne Ottinger, Pauline Shirley, John J. Perry, Jim Blasingame, Beverly Williams, Willa Robinson, Addie Richmond, William M. Causey, William R. Branch, Edward C. Blesi, Valerie Perea, Donald Trautner, Bennie Bough, Tom Grady, Art Jackson, Cynthia Young, Stella Guerra Nelson, Bobbie Garza, Gwendolyn Talbot, Dilip Abayasekara, James Whelan, Roxanne Pruski, Dottie Walters, Marshall Lewis, Dolly Ogawa, Joan Cassidy, Arlene Kushner, Becky Sigler, Reba and P. T. Eichelberger, Muriel Yilmaz, Jo Reynolds, Mary Jane and Neal Brigham have assisted in a variety of ways.

My gratitude extends to family members who were understanding and supportive: James and Laurie Ellis, Resa and Arlon Motsch, Thomas and Patti Ellis, Michael and Jenni Ellis, Susan and Ronald Hodges, Brenda Neilson, Joseph and Mary Ellen Donatto, Geri Collins, Fred Founteno, and Nora LaChepelle.

Warning-Disclaimer

This book is designed to provide information in regard to the subject matter covered. It is sold with the understanding that the publisher and author are not engaged in rendering legal, accounting, or other professional services. If counseling or other expert assistance is required, the services of a competent professional should be sought.

It is not the purpose of this primer to reprint all the information that is otherwise available to the author and/or publisher, but to complement, amplify and supplement other texts. You are urged to read all the available material, learn as much as possible about the subject matter and to tailor the information to your individual needs. For more information, see the many references in Selected Readings.

Every effort has been made to make this book as accurate as possible. However, there may be mistakes both typographical and in content. Therefore, this text should be used only as a general guide and not as the ultimate source of information.

The purpose of this book is to educate and to entertain. The author and GoalMinds® shall have neither liability nor responsibility to any person or entity with respect to any loss or damage caused, or alleged to be caused, directly or indirectly by the information contained in this book.

If you do not wish to be bound by the above, you may return this book to the publisher for a full refund.

Introduction

What can you possibly achieve within the foreseeable future? Do you dare to think of it?

This book is meant to stimulate your thinking. It should be read with your pen in hand. Doodle on the edges of the pages. Record your thoughts. Siphon off time to dream while you are awake. Take time to think and do the exercises.

The key to making progress is in transferring ideas from your mind, through your fingers, to a fixed state so you can consider the ideas again and again. Repetition! Repetition! Spaced repetition locks the messages into the subconscious.

The process presented here works with little effort, but knowing the process is of little use unless you take action. Record your progress on the back of an envelope, or on your computer. Use any program manager software, a daily planner, or a journal.

We can be satisfied with so little, when we were created for greatness and abundance. What are our limits? We often create them for ourselves, finding excuses, accepting victimhood, and giving up on what might have been.

It's risky, of course, reaching higher. People may laugh at you, trying to pull you back. You may make a mistake and stumble and fall. However, you will never know how high you can climb if you cling to the first steps just because they are secure. You can convince yourself you are satisfied. Like the servant in the Bible, you might bury your talent.

The process presented in this book has been used by many to achieve extraordinary results. I have personally used it to move from relative poverty to financial security, to move from self-consciousness to self-confidence, to move from being one of the crowd to high profile leadership positions. You may not aspire to leadership positions. You might even prefer a place in the wilderness! The process will work for you just the same. I challenge you, no matter what it is you want in life, to rise up, take the risks, and dare to stumble; pick yourself up and try again. At stake, is the beautiful, wonderful, powerful person you are.

*The greatest achievement
was at first and for a time
a dream.
The oak sleeps in the acorn;
the bird waits in the egg;
and in the highest vision of
the soul a waking angel stirs.
Dreams are the seedlings
of realities.*

—James Allen

SECTION ONE

Envision Your Future

Chapter 1

Dream Great Dreams

If you could be anything you want to be, what would you be? If you could do anything you want to do, what would you do? If you could have anything you want to have, what would you have? If you were to design the life you want to be living ten years from now, what would it be like? You can make it happen.

There is no straight line from where you are to where you want to be. Life is not a linear process with steps following each other. Rather, it is an intricate weaving back and forth, in and out, of dreaming, planning, rewarding, enrolling, analyzing, evaluating. The most effective route I have found is reading, learning from others, and setting my sights high. Once set upon something, commitment, determination, and persistence can take over. The difference between success and a near miss is often knowing when to be flexible and when to stand firm.

At the beginning of the 1990 conflict in the Middle East, I was a deputy division chief at Army Headquarters in the Pentagon. One of my prime projects was to establish a logistics planning cell to support the emergency operations center. We took the longer view, planning the next days and weeks while the operation center dealt with immediate actions. We worked up agendas with the director and attended the mastermind meetings of the leaders of various segments of the armed forces and civilian agencies as they anticipated requirements, reviewed policies, and directed actions in various parts of the world. The nerve center of the Army is an exciting place for a civilian to be.

In 1991, I was elected leader of a 3,000 member non-profit organization in the Washington, DC, area, District 27 of Toastmasters International. At the end of my year in office, we ranked #1 in that worldwide organization. It had never happened in the DC area before. Sometime later it was said that I was the only person who could have accomplished that. It was my "personality." That was a misperception. It was then that I began analyzing what had taken place and writing it down. I was convinced that anyone with basic leadership skills could do what I had done if they knew the process I had used. I shared this process with other leaders and they, too, produced extraordinary results.

Three ministers out on a lake one Sunday afternoon, fishing and relaxing, illustrate my point. One of the ministers said, "I think I'll go for a little walk." He stood up, stretched, stepped out of the boat and began to walk on the water. The other ministers sat in the boat and smiled at each other. Then a second minister stood and said, "I think I'll join him." Out he stepped and began walking across the water. By this time, the third minister was not to be outdone. He reasoned, "My faith is every bit as strong as theirs." Standing, he stretched and stepped over the side of the boat. He immediately disappeared. After a few seconds, he surfaced, sputtering, gasping and grabbing air. Then down he went again. The second time he came up he was kicking wildly, his arms flailing. He was trying to find the side of the boat—but not soon enough—

> *"Everything is possible to one who has faith."*
> —Bible, Mark 9:23

down he went. One of the ministers who had been standing on the water looked at the other and said calmly, "Don't you think we should tell him where the rocks are?"

You can be anything you want to be. You can do anything you want to do. You can have anything you want to have, if you know what you want and are willing to pay the price. This primer presents some stepping stones for you.

> **Take Charge**
> *Think of possibilities.*
> *Plot your course.*
> *Take action.*

Chapter 2

Define Your Terms

The first step toward a spectacular future is to create a vivid vision of what you want it to be. A spectacular future may be becoming the Chief Executive Officer of a giant corporation. It may be leaving the corporate world to build a business of your own. It may be raising a family and forgoing a career in the business world. The choice is yours.

A vivid vision is different from an apparition or a hallucination. But a lot of us have difficulty deciding just what that vision is. We expect our leaders to have it; we know it when we see it, but it is hard to define. Let's put it in context.

VISION: Seeing what might be, and believing that it can be. Wrapped in values, principles and beliefs, vision arouses passions and causes us to take action. Vision is a force that drives us, entices us, and leads us to make real what we once only imagined.

The winner of the 1996 Indianapolis 500 auto race had a vision. His body was broken with fractures, bone chips, and exposed nerves, yet he raced. He had had a vision for several years seeing himself as the champion. When he won the race that day, he said simply, "I gave it all I had."

> *"It is far better to be pulled by a vision than to be pushed by circumstances."*
> —John J. Perry

DREAMS: As used here, are those wide-awake mental excursions that we periodically take into other realms. These dreams are fleeting, often fanciful, ideas of optimum satisfaction or pleasure. Thoughts flowing from our creative imaginations, dreams are raw material for visions.

MISSION: A clear, definable and motivational point of focus, it is an achievable goal, a finish line to work toward. Your current mission may be a step toward the realization of your vision.

While your vision may see you as a famous surgeon, your current mission would be to become a reputable physician.

PURPOSE: The fundamental set of reasons for our existence. It is a stabilizing, long-term reason for being.

Mother Theresa of Calcutta's reason for being seemed to be to take care of the poorest of the poor in India. What is your purpose in life? What is your reason for living? Think about it.

SUCCESS: A life well lived, from the inside out, fully awake and aware of the choices we make and the consequences of those choices.

> *Put It In Context*
> *When is a dream not a dream?*
> *Think about your purpose in life.*

Chapter 3

Take Time to Think

You are creating the person you will become by the way you envision that person, the goals you set and the actions you take. By exercising your free will and consciously making choices, you become co-creator with the Maker of all things.

Do you want to go to graduate school or take fun courses? Do you get involved in social work or climb the social ladder? These are not right or wrong or even mutually exclusive decisions, but they do lead in different directions. If we are creating the persons we will become, shouldn't we think about what we are doing now, why we are doing it, and where it is leading us? We need to raise our level of awareness.

Do a Lifeline Exercise

A lifeline exercise which is frequently used in career planning and management might be useful here to "see" graphically how your life looks, to gain insight into your world view, to chart relationship patterns, and to consider your future.

The usual lifeline extends from birth to death. However, in many cultures, more subtle perhaps in the western world, career is discussed, predicted and planned by family and community well before the birth of the child. Acknowledging this reality and addressing it will help us separate a personal vision from that of our family or community. This is not always an easy or comfortable task. We see this influence in some military families with several generations of military leaders. The first-born, particularly, senses some expectation that he or she will follow the family tradition.

Extending the lifeline to some years past our death challenges us to consider our "legacy." What do we hope to leave? What contribution do we wish to make? What are we REALLY working toward? Donna Holley has used this exercise with undergraduate and graduate business students. "It is a useful tool for students to 'see' what 'work life' has been for them and to chart their dreams and dreads about their career into the future."

Expand the scope of this exercise and consider life in general. A model is provided for your use on page 42, where you will be challenged to identify significant events of your life and chart them using Donna Holley's model. Events considered "positive" are usually noted above the line and those considered difficult or "negative" below the line. Then think about the future by predicting significant events that will take place between now and some years (perhaps ten) after your death. Such events might involve aging parents, graduation, promotion, birth, death of a loved one, and so on.

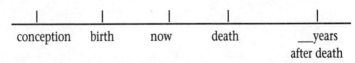

Donna J. Holley, M.Ed.MSW, 1999, Lifeline Extensions. Used with permission.

"The best use of life is to spend it for something that outlasts life."

—William James

Ask yourself: To what extent are my choices today influenced by past events? What direction is my life taking? What influences my choices?

Review Your Life Story

Using the lifeline will make it easier to look at your recent past. What have you accomplished? Look for experiences that might reveal successes in the types of things you will be attempting in the future. Make a list. This will indicate some of your strengths. What do you need to improve upon with more education or experience? Perhaps you should take an aptitude test or a preference test, which would indicate a natural leaning toward some activity. It is easier to achieve in areas where you have a head start with natural ability.

Examine your current situation. What will you accomplish this year if you keep doing what you are now doing? Look for trends. How will that help you realize your dream? What if you do nothing differently, that is, you do not have the time, energy or money to do anything else? What if you decided now to take charge of your life by taking responsibility for how it turns out?

> *"Some people die at twenty-five and are not buried until they are seventy-five."*
> —Benjamin Franklin

Look at Your Personal Rule Book

Reflect upon the lifeline exercise. You may discover how certain values have influenced your life. Values are the criteria by which we evaluate our behavior and the behavior of others. They are the things which anchor us in this world and give us parameters within which we operate. Our values are the qualities we feel make life worth living. They influence key aspects of our lives, such as personal satisfaction, major decisions and life goals. Is honesty important to you? Are personal discipline, integrity, loyalty, financial independence, family and community important? What about belief in yourself, loving relationships with others, and a higher power? Are they important to you? Take a moment to make a list of your values. Ask yourself, "What do I stand for?" Try to surface the values you are not likely to change, your core values.

Now think about your life and the choices you have made. Do these reflect what you value most in life? A look at your values can help you predict your future. The choices you make in the future will probably be guided by those same values, unless you consciously decide to begin to adopt new values.

Know What You Don't Want

It has been said that the great Italian sculptor, Michelangelo, when asked how he could carve such marvelous works in the marble, replied that he only chipped the excess stone away from the form already inside the marble. He apparently was thinking of what he did not want in a very positive manner. He was focused on the unfolding figure in the marble. So, too, it may be with you. Dreaming may be less difficult if you begin with what you do not want. What unnecessary obstacles can you chip away that will reveal your vision?

> *"Thinking always of trying to do more brings a state of mind in which nothing seems impossible."*
> —Henry Ford

> I do not want to risk everything and end up on welfare.
>
> I do not want to move to another state.
>
> I do not want to lose my spouse.
>
> I do not want to miss any of my children's sporting events.
>
> I do not want to work outside my home.

There was a young man in the slums who decided his obstacle was living in the streets. "I had a vision," he told a conference in Switzerland, "of seeing my 30th birthday." He was tough, but the streets were tougher. Ron was thankful that he had never left anyone "breathless." He was not a murderer. He dreamed of something extraordinary for young people in his neighborhood. Few lived to reach the age of 30. A caring teacher had encouraged him to get off drugs and make a better life for himself. He went into rehabilitation and began to do some blue-sky thinking. He could see possibilities and took action to change his circumstances.

> *"We live in the present, we dream of the future, but we learn eternal truths from the past."*
> —Madame Chiang Kai-shek

By stating what you don't want, you may begin to set up parameters, boundaries on your dreams. These lead to a controlled imagination. The fewer boundaries we set, the more free-flowing our ideas. After considering what you don't want, think of your dream in a positive sense. What do you want?

> **Take Time to Reflect**
> *Anchor yourself in core values.*
> *Extraordinary achievement*
> *requires personal discipline.*

Chapter 4

Use Your Creative Imagination

Think! Daydream! What's possible? Go a little bit crazy! Give yourself permission to let go of reality for a time.

Let down the boundaries you've been living within and look over the horizon with a wide-angle lens. You have the power within you right now to achieve anything you want to achieve, to become anything you want to be! How can you be satisfied with the status quo, the current state of things, when the world is filled with abundance and you have talents to be used?

Imagine!

What if you won the $10 million dollar lottery? What would you do differently? Winning is out of your control, but thinking about it may lead you to think of the things you do want in life. And, if you want them badly enough, you are capable of devising ways to have them. Stretch your mind.

My friend, Barbara, dreamed of eradicating world hunger. She had no international connections, no political clout, nor is she a leader in a non-profit organization whose mission it is to feed the hungry. She soon found out that this dream was truly out of reach for her.

It is fine to begin with outlandish notions. As you will see, you can very quickly discover whether are not they are things you could expect to achieve.

The first objective is to break out of the routine. Look ahead and stretch your imagination. Later on you can analyze your dreams and decide whether or not to pursue them.

Explore Possibilities

How long has it been since you have had a bright idea? Not necessarily one that worked—just an innovative idea that caused you to take action? We can become more creative by adopting a creative attitude and actively developing new habits like asking "what if" questions and looking beyond the first answer.

In July 1997, the spacecraft, Pathfinder, landed on Mars while scientists at the Jet Propulsion Laboratory in Pasadena, CA, cheered. An earth-born robot operating on Mars? Impossible! Unthinkable! "Get creative. Think outside the box," the NASA administrator told the scientists. Build a spacecraft in one-fourth the time, at one- fourth the cost of earlier space missions. They did.

Boundaries? Restrictions? Stay within the boxes? No! Something new was needed. The vision, the challenge, the dream! They were all there.

Thirty years earlier, President John F. Kennedy had visualized Americans going to the moon and back. He challenged space scientists to make it happen within a decade. Ten years! No one knew how it could be done, but they set about doing it.

> *"Imagination is more important than knowledge."*
> —Albert Einstein

Kenneth Levin and his group of engineers at Bell

Aero Systems in Niagara Falls, NY, had a bright idea. That idea developed into a lunar landing research vehicle that could fly on the earth just as it would on the moon, but in only a one-sixth gravitational field compared to the earth's gravity. In addition, it flew as though it was in a vacuum, just like on the moon. Levin found a partner for his efforts at Bell. The NASA Flight Research Center had independently proposed a very similar approach during the same period Levin was developing his idea at Bell. Together, Bell and NASA got the job done. The research and training that this vehicle provided solved the most difficult task that the astronauts had to perform on the entire Apollo mission, that of making the lunar landing. Within nine years, astronauts had traversed the 240,000 miles to the moon, walked on it, and returned home safely. Dreams!

NASA Dryden

Aspiring to do more or better is not foolish at all. It is a matter of knowing what you want. If you truly would like to stretch the possibilities of your life and establish more ambitious goals, then you must be bold enough to dream great dreams.

Expand Your Thinking

Most of us don't use our creativity because we're locked into habits and thought patterns that we assumed as we were growing up, patterns like always looking for the one right answer. Admonitions such as "be logical," "be practical," and "don't rock the boat" have stifled our imaginations. Those admonitions may have been well intended, but they do not lead to living more creative lives. Many people still believe that you have to be a little bit crazy to be creative!

Forget the restrictions. You are shopping for possibilities. Look at audacious and outrageous, seemingly impossible ideas.

Stretch your imagination. Blue-sky thinking is similar to what some scholars call the ideate stage of the process cycle, or "shopping for options." There will be time for evaluating the ideas later on. That is when we become logical and analyze, evaluate, and meditate on our dreams.

> *"I always wanted to be somebody, but I should have been more specific!"*
> —Lilly Tomlin

Have Fun

For now, have fun. Dream! Focus on the majesty and excitement of what might be. Use your creative imagination. Go for the big picture. Do not be afraid to be outrageous. Dare to dream the impossible dreams. Who's to say what is impossible anyway?

> ***Relax and Be Receptive***
> *Allow new thoughts to enter your mind.*
> *Be playful with ideas.*

Chapter 5

Design Your future

Find a peaceful place and relax. (Some prefer the same place, one especially set aside for thinking.) This may take only a few moments here and there, or it may take days. Free your mind from everyday thoughts to allow space for new ideas. It is not easy, but with practice it will become easier and more fruitful. Breathe deeply and evenly. Then begin to think of the future as you would like it to be.

Look at the Big Picture

Consider all aspects of your life. There may be many things you want: financial security, physical health, loving relationships and family life, spiritual well being, career progression. A vision is a long term objective marked by intermediate milestones. In the long term there will be many opportunities to focus on specific areas of your life. First, spend some time developing a composite picture of the future "you." Then select one area and begin to practice these techniques. This is not a linear process, remember, but a dynamic leaping forward and sometimes looping back, evaluating, dreaming, rewarding, planning.

Ask yourself: What is the best I can be? How can I become a better person, parent, spouse, or whatever I want to become? What would a life of abundance mean to me?

Asking questions helps guide your imagination along specific paths. Lift your sights and look at the stars. Look around you at those who are succeeding at what you would like to achieve. Look within your heart and ask yourself, "Why can't I?"

This productive dreaming has the capacity to become a powerful force in your life.

It can:

    Generate positive expectations

    Make change more acceptable

    Boost self-confidence

    Provide direction

    Unlock energy

Find Time to Dream

There will never seem to be enough time for daydreaming. Life is already full of things we must do. How can we siphon off time to get away from it all? We must decide to take time to look for spare moments. For instance, what is your mind doing while you brush your teeth? Could you sneak in a moment to think about your future? What do you do while stuck in traffic or in the line at the supermarket? Manage your mind. Why not drift off into some blue-sky thinking or guided imagining? Our thoughts are the only things we can completely control. It just takes a little awareness and practice, which may mean forming some new habits.

> *"You must learn to be still in the midst of activity and to be vibrantly alive in repose."*
>
>   – Indira Gandhi

Stop Muddling Through

Too often we find ourselves muddling through day by day, complaining about our circumstances. Maybe you can't change those circumstances this week or even this year. If you look ahead, though, you quite possibly could change those circumstances within two years. The key is to begin now to think about it and find a way.

Think without the parameters you set earlier. Let your mind wander, daydream. What do you want out of life? Write down your thoughts. Then at another time, do some creative thinking within the parameters you set. Write down those thoughts. Then compare the two. You may find that the differences are only obstacles, which can be worked around. Set your mind free. Ideas will come to you. Then use your creative imagination to build on those ideas. Let your dream move you.

Eric Weihenmayer lost his sight when he was a child as a result of a rare disease. But he never lost his vision. He has a lifetime filled with goals. Eric explained, "I want to make it in a sighted world." In 1995, this math and English teacher, who also coaches his school's wrestling club, successfully climbed Mt. McKinley, the highest peak in North America.

Transform Your Dream

Take the next step and transform those dreams into a vision of the future. This vision should incorporate all aspects of your life. It might include a dream home, loving family members, good physical and mental health, and financial stability.

When you decide to pursue your dreams, your life may seem out of balance for a while. You will be focused more strongly on one particular goal or another. For instance, you may need a college degree in order to move on to other goals. For awhile, that task would take priority, while other goals wait their turn. This often happens when an important project requires a lot of extra effort. If you have your eyes on the vision, you will know that these efforts are aimed at an end point. It is easier to accept being out of balance when you know that it is only a temporary condition, and when you acknowledge that the goal is worth the effort.

> *"Whatever you can do, or dream you can, begin it. Boldness has genius, power, and magic in it."*
> – Goethe

Discover the Power

It is possible that the energy of our dreams can truly affect the world about us. There are many who are convinced that this is so. Norman Vincent Peale said the universe is like a giant echo chamber; sooner or later what you send out comes back to you. Quantum physicists tell us how the expectations of an observer can actually change the behavior of particles. It is not unreasonable to think that your expectations can change your environment as well as yourself.

Proceed with Caution

When you find a dream about which you are passionate, analyze and evaluate it before running with it.

Chasing a dream is a personal process. We cannot have a vision for others and hope to change their lives.

We must focus on ourselves. Others will be affected by what we want to happen, but we can only control our own thoughts.

> *All things are possible to those who believe.*
> Look inward.
> Dream first, then evaluate.

ADDITIONAL RESOURCES:
Positive Imaging, Norman Vincent Peale
Blue-Sky Thinking, Daniel Jingwa
A Whack on the Side of the Head, Roger Von Oech

YOUR TURN – TAKE ACTION

Dream Great Dreams

1. Spend some time doing a lifeline exercise. Plot positive events above the line and negative events below the line. Begin at pre-birth and continue to ten years after death. Consider family life before your birth and the legacy you will leave. Refer back to Chapter 3 if you would like to refresh your memory.

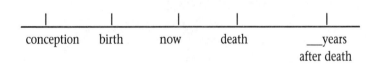

conception   birth   now   death   ___years after death

2. What are your dreams?
_____
_____
_____
_____
_____

_____
_____
_____
_____
_____
_____
_____

3. Are they consistent with your values, beliefs, and purpose?

	____ Yes ____ Not sure ____ No

4. If not, how does that affect your thinking?
_____
_____
_____
_____
_____
_____
_____
_____
_____

5. What qualities do you now have to help achieve the dream?
_____
_____
_____

6. What additional qualities, if any, are needed to achieve the dream?

7. What has been your greatest success to date?

8. What did you accomplish last year?

Think of Possibilities!

In the long run we shape our lives, and we shape ourselves. The process never ends until we die. And the choices we make are ultimately our own responsibility.

– Eleanor Roosevelt

SECTION TWO

Make a Conscious Decision

Chapter 6

Exercise Your Power to Choose

Simply dreaming great dreams will not change your life; although, it is a first step in getting what you want. What do you do with these dreams? How could they possibly become reality? What would it take?

Many factors need to be considered so that you can make an informed decision whether or not to take action on these great ideas. Sift your dreams, your right brain, imaginative thinking, through the logical sieve of the left brain. That will lead you to a reasoned course of action. We form the dream in the right hemisphere of our brain, but the left hemisphere has to believe that the dream is do-able, in the realm of possibility. This allows a belief to be born and from that belief, a vision is born. The subconscious mind can then help us make it happen.

Visions are internal gyroscopes, guiding us in the direction of the person we want to become. They pull us in the direction of our desired outcome while we make daily decisions. When faced with choices, instead of thinking in terms of today or tomorrow, we are more inclined to look to the future and ask ourselves what those choices will mean in the long run. A vision is a dream that you feel is reachable, even if it seems outrageous.

Analyze the Dream You Selected

Many of us overlook the process of analyzing and jump right into action when we have a bright idea.

Analysis is a key area that can make life work a lot better for us. By analyzing the possibilities and perils associated with a dream, we are in a better position to evaluate the potential effects. This is no easy task. Bringing dreams into reality takes effort.

One of my associates, a successful lawyer in Washington, DC, stopped off for a few days in Hawaii while returning from a trip to Japan. She was so impressed with the wonderful people she met that she was unhappy when she returned to Washington. There she resumed her "rat race" routine, working long hours and commuting in rush hour traffic. She reminisced about what she had experienced in Hawaii and quickly decided to return there to live. She gave up her practice, sold most of her belongings, and moved. Shortly after settling into her new surroundings, she discovered flying bugs, wind, and other annoyances. She had not considered the challenge of starting over or the length of time it took to reach the mainland where she still needed to conduct business. She had acted too hastily. Reality turned her dream into a nightmare. She just did not understand the power of her personal choices.

Evaluate

The dream can only become reality when a conscious and whole-hearted choice is made to follow that dream. Our task is to analyze and evaluate the product of our creative imagination. Find a dream and take positive action to make it happen.

> *"You don't just luck into things...You build step by step, whether it's friendships or opportunities."*
>
> – Barbara Bush

Think of your dream and try to envision any obstacles that might interfere with its success. Often it seems like circumstances are hiding along our path, waiting to trip us. Turn over the rocks and see what is standing in your way. Look at the obstacles, hurdles that will have to be overcome. Maybe you dream of becoming a surgeon. What will it take? More education, more money, more time and energy? Are these things that could prevent you from achieving your dream? Think of ways you could overcome those obstacles.

Look at the risks. What do you have to lose? On the other hand, what resources do you already have? Perhaps you already have a related degree and savings or investments to cover costs. What benefits will come from this effort for you and others? Most of all, in the final analysis, you must develop a belief in your dream and in yourself.

Make a Decision

In every single decision we make, there is power – the power to shape and control our own lives. Unfortunately, most of the time we do not realize or understand how powerful we really are. Instead of pursuing our own empowerment, we sometimes blame our choices on outside influences. We speak in terms of what acted on us to cause a situation. How many times have you heard someone say, "I had no choice," or I couldn't help it?" Was it true? Or did the person just not understand the power of his or her personal choices?

> *"The block of granite which was an obstacle in the pathway of the weak becomes a stepping stone in the pathway of the strong."*
>
> – Thomas Carlyle

Every day we make dozens, if not hundreds, of decisions. Some of them are fairly routine: what we will eat for breakfast, what we will wear, what radio station we will listen to. Some involve work: how to answer a letter, when to place a call. Other decisions touch our personal lives: whom to date, whom to marry, should we buy a house or move to a new city?

When I decided to move from Texas to the Washington, DC, area, my friends found it hard to believe. "Leave Texas?" "Do you know about the crime rate in DC...and all that traffic?" "It SNOWS up there!" Yes, I had considered all that and the benefits, too. When I arrived in the DC area, I was met with, "You left Texas to come up here???" However, my career opportunities were greater in DC. There was crime where I lived in Texas, too. Traffic may be worse in the DC area, but I could learn to deal with it.

My vision was living a life of ease in my senior years, and my career move was in line with that vision. It turned out to be an excellent decision. I eventually landed a promotion in the Pentagon and spent several very challenging and exciting years there.

Know Your Power
Use the process to
help you choose.

Chapter 7

Reach for A Dream Catcher

Before you decide to act on your dream, put it through an evaluation process. Think of the dream, the outcome you envision. Take time to think carefully about all aspects of it and to gather information.

Have you ever seen a dream catcher? Members of the Sioux Nation are said to believe a dream catcher only allows good dreams to come through to us.

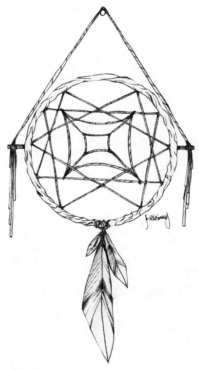

The dream catcher is fashioned from a twig. Webbing, like a spider web, is slipped over the twig. The twig is bent and fastened to form a circle. A feather is tied to the center of the webbing, and usually other feathers are attached to the twig. Ribbons are sometimes tied with the feathers. The dream catcher is usually placed over or near the bed.

According to legend, at night when dreams come to those in the room with a dream catcher, good dreams slip through the webbing, slide down the feathers and stay with the dreamer. Bad dreams, however, don't know the way through the webbing and get caught. At first light of day, the bad dreams dissipate and are gone.

We can use an imaginary dream catcher (our thought process) to process our dreams. The webbing can separate obstacles, risks, resources, and benefits, so that we can look more closely at the dreams. Having examined them, we can then determine which should slip through the webbing. These are the ones we want to commit to action.

My dream catchers remind me to look around the blocks of granite along my path and scan the horizon for potential obstacles and risks. They also help keep me focused on the good dreams that slip through the webbing.

> ***Separate Emotion from Logic***
> *Examine your dreams.*
> *Turn them over and look at the other side.*
> *Decide with your eyes wide open.*

Chapter 8

Evaluate the Dream

What are the Risks?

The word "risk" is hard to define. Risks are sometimes even harder to identify. Think of a risk as a gamble. It is an event that we do not control, a chance we take. There is a possibility that things will turn out okay, but there is also the chance of a threat to our plans. Some people risk blindly, jumping into things with their eyes closed, hoping for the best. If you recognize the risks and evaluate them in advance, then move ahead, you are taking a calculated risk.

There may be a loss of funds if the venture fails, or a temporary decrease in expendable income as you invest. There may also be embarrassment if you put yourself on the line for something that does not succeed. You may even have to listen to people say, "I told you so!"

You may risk losing friends or putting a strain on family relationships if your dream involves major changes in lifestyle or circumstances that cause you not to be as available as you were before. Fear of success is an unspoken fear for many high achieving individuals. Some fear they will surpass their families. Their interests will change; they will grow farther from them economically and socially. Yet, many don't take the time to consider what that means and how to cope with this problem if it does occur.

To refuse to make a decision is to make a decision.

When a concern is ignored and allowed to continue to nag, it drains off energy and enthusiasm. It is best to face the concern or fear squarely and decide how to handle the situation early on. There may be things that you can do to prevent it from happening.

For example, you may take those loved ones into your confidence and allow them to feel a part of your adventure. You might even hire some of them. On the other hand, if they have no interest in participating and are reluctant about seeing you make changes in your life that could affect how they relate to you, you then have another choice to make.

Look for Potential Obstacles and Solutions

Obstacles make life interesting! They are detriments to some who see only the blockage in their paths. To others, an obstacle is simply a stumbling block that can be overcome with foresight and diligence. It is an opportunity to improve yourself and the situation. An optimistic attitude is important. The person who succeeds is the one who knows how to turn a problem inside out, so that it becomes the genesis for a solution.

Jay is one of those fortunate people who knew early in life what he wanted to be when he grew up. Before he graduated from high school Jay knew he wanted a career in law enforcement.

First obstacle: Upon graduating from high school, Jay was too young to be considered by local law enforcement agencies.

> *"The greater the obstacle, the greater the glory in overcoming it."*
> – Ralph Smedley

Solution: Go to college. He enrolled in law enforcement classes. Result: That only fired him up more. After the first semester, he had a powerful urge to get out and "do it."

Obstacle: Jay was still too young to be considered for the local police force, much less state police forces.

Solution: Check out opportunities with the military services. Jay discovered that not only would the Army guarantee him the law enforcement career field, they would send him to his first choice for an assignment, Germany. After that assignment, he did a "hardship tour" in Hawaii! Then he was old enough to pursue his dream in local law enforcement. Result: He passed the necessary examinations easily.

Jay could have bided his time until he became old enough. He could have said, "Well, maybe not being old enough was a sign that law enforcement was not for me." He could have gone into another career. Instead, he had "fixity" of purpose. He envisioned his future and was determined to have it.

Explore Options

When you know what you want, but are unsure of your skills, spend time upgrading them.

This is "working around" a problem or challenge. For example, you need computer skills and you only know

> "Behold the turtle. He makes progress only when he sticks his neck out."
>
> –James Bryant Conant

the basics. You can upgrade these skills by taking classes, even adult classes at night. If childcare is an obstacle, you might trade off with someone else who needs childcare services. Another possibility might be to ask a friend or relative who already has the necessary skills to help you.

Maybe you need a car to get to classes or a new job. How can you get around that obstacle? Car pool, take the bus, ride your bicycle...think creatively!

You need $500,000 start-up capital. Is that obstacle insurmountable? Where are the potential resources? A small business loan? A financial broker? An investment banker?

Estimate the Costs

Nothing comes without a cost. There could also be a down side to your dream.

Ask yourself if there is a price to be paid for going ahead with the dream. You may have less time for your family or friends. It may be necessary to temporarily abandon leisure activities you have enjoyed. Perhaps you have a spouse who is not supportive of this venture and will be unhappy with you if you proceed.

> *"Knowledge is the only kind of wealth that multiplies when you give it away."*
> –Peter Schwartz

Investing yourself in a major venture requires energy. You may be more tired if you put in long hours and more subject to stress if things go wrong. If you are investing money, you may be committing some or all of your savings.

Identify Resources

What are the resources you can rely upon as you work to fulfill the dream?

Your venture will require an investment. Perhaps funds will be required to underwrite your vision. Do you have capital? Can you borrow it? Are others, with whom you are working, willing to invest? Or is the organization or company you are working for prepared to see this through?

Are material resources available, such as computers, software and office space?

But most important of all, what are the human resources you will be able to rely upon? The human investment in a venture involves time, energy, technical expertise, and a willingness to learn and develop on your part and the part of associates.

Another resource is the guidance and wisdom of others who have walked similar paths. Will you be able to find such people to advise you? What will it cost?

Find the Benefits

Ask yourself what the potential benefits would be for yourself, for others who would work with you, and for those who would be recipients of what you hope to provide.

There may be a payoff in financial profits. This may give you a new sense of security and allow you to enjoy such things as travel and more leisure time.

> *"If all difficulties were known at the outset of a long journey, most of us would never start out at all."*
> – Dan Rather

You almost certainly will achieve personal growth and gain new insights.

Maybe you will become a stronger, more self-confident person. You may have a chance to meet new and exciting people.

You may have a one-time opportunity to embark on an adventure that provides its own high.

It may also be that your reward will come as a sense of satisfaction and achievement. Perhaps you will be left with a realization that you have done something constructive in this world–provided a service or made life easier for others. Think of the legacy you will leave.

You can achieve extraordinary things if you know what you want and decide to work to have it.

Analyze the Dream
Look for risks and obstacles.
Think of solutions.
Consider resources.
Consider benefits.

Chapter 9

Practice "What If" Drills

In business we have contingency management, "con-man." For the Army we wrote and exercised contingency plans. In our personal lives, we should also consider in advance those times when life throws us a curve, when things don't go the way we planned it. One very useful technique is to do mental "what if" drills in order to anticipate obstacles. Use your "over the horizon" radar. Run different scenarios through your mind. Large companies hire people simply to gather information, "look into the future," and think up plausible scenarios of what the company may face in the future. The company is then able to do contingency planning. You can benefit from those techniques, too.

Think up several scenarios that are plausible for you. Let's say it is now ten years into the future. You have earned your Masters Degree in Business Administration (MBA). It took a lot of sacrifices. You delayed marriage, vacations, and the car of your dreams. Now, the student loans are paid off, you have a spouse, and you have decided to buy a very nice house in the country. You are starting a family and what if:

> Your parents suddenly become your dependents
>
> You hate your job and want to quit
>
> One of your major investments goes sour just when you need the money for the house

Contemplate these obstacles and brainstorm some possible solutions with a trusted friend. Anticipating obstacles and thinking of possible solutions prepares you to deal with the situation more decisively when problems occur. Develop some mental contingency plans. If...Then...If this happens, then here is how I will get around that. If that happens, I will need to do this.

Ask Others

"What am I missing?" If your dream seems too good to be true, no obstacles, it probably is too good to be true! Your judgment may be clouded by your emotions. Ask a trusted friend to help you think it through. Step back and take an objective, more analytical look. Now is the time to narrow your focus and "go deep."

"What if" drills will boost your confidence. Even if the challenging events you encounter are not the precise scenario you thought up, you will have practice in creative problem solving. "Stuff happens." But looking "over the horizon," anticipating, and doing "what if" drills will reassure you that you are prepared. There is no need to panic. There is a solution out there somewhere, and you know you can handle it.

Ask Yourself:

- Is the dream worth it?

- Do the gains outweigh the costs?

- Am I willing to pay the price?

- Am I satisfied that I can find solutions to overcome anticipated obstacles?

- Do I have confidence in my skills and in the possibility of my dream?

Obviously, if you have answered "YES" to these questions, you have begun to turn your dream into a vision. But what if you haven't answered "YES" right down the line? Maybe your spouse has told you he will leave you if you spend too much time on business; perhaps you have a history of heart problems and stress is bad for you. This is where value judgments become most important. You will want to think long and hard about what it all means to you.

If your dream starts to feel like a burden, if you suspect that it may cost too much, then perhaps the dream should remain just that, a dream. The choice is yours.

Weigh the Options

Be grateful that you know what is most important in life for you. If you come to the conclusion that your dream should not be pursued at this time, take a deep breath and let it go without regrets. In your decisiveness, you have shown strength. Look for another dream.

If you recognize that this dream truly is of major importance to you, then there is no need to rush to give up. There may yet be ways to make it work. Perhaps you simply need to reframe it, modifying the goals and making its scope more modest. Possibly you need to take additional time before putting it into action. That's very different from abandoning it.

"As is our confidence, so is our capacity."
–William Hazlitt

There are those who recommend doing a quantitative analysis in order to help you decide if you should move ahead with your dream. Each factor is given a numerical weight and counted as negative or positive. If the negatives weigh more, add up to the greater number, the decision is against moving ahead. If the positives add up to the greater number, the decision is to move ahead. If such an approach feels right for you, then by all means do it! It may provide you with an important tool for making a decision.

Try It On

I was being interviewed about communication skills on a cable television show, when one of the hosts switched the topic to this book. The co-hosts shared a dream of becoming hosts on a major network TV show. They were quite excited about the idea as they thought of the glamour, the celebrity status, the perks. They wanted my help in discovering the next step for them.

The co-hosts and I talked about putting the dream through the dream catcher. What were potential obstacles? First, they would probably have a very early morning show and neither liked getting up in the morning. They would probably have to move to New York or commute long distances, which might create risks in their marriages. Although the benefits included fame, fortune and other perks, after very brief consideration, they both decided that this was not what they wanted in life. By taking time to seriously consider the wish they each held, they were able to see it was not

> *No pain, no palm; no thorn, no throne; no gall, no glory; no cross, no crown."*
> – William Penn

what they really wanted, and let it go. They could have spent a lot of time saying, "If only...." Instead, they asked themselves, "What if...?" They did the best possible thing and analyzed their dream.

They quickly put the idea of a major network program behind them and left the show just as excited as they had been about the idea in the beginning. The difference was that they were now excited about finding a new dream and putting it through the filter of a dream catcher.

> **Think in terms of "Con-Man" Contingency Management**
> *Focus on the future.*
> *Look around the periphery.*
> *Keep thinking of solutions.*

Chapter 10

Make a Commitment

When all the analysis is done, what matters most is if your gut says, "go with it," and if a voice in your head is saying, "I can do it." Without that message, that inner confidence and drive, the numbers will mean little. As Carl Jung advised, "Your vision will become clear only when you look into your heart. Who looks outside, dreams. Who looks inside, awakens."

Look Inside

The decision to go with your dream is what gives you the power to turn it into reality. It is a conscious decision, taken with full commitment and responsibility. And, it is crucial to everything that will follow. Without that conscious decision, it will be easy to cave in at the first obstacle you encounter. But once you have made the decision, you have internalized it and made it part of yourself. It will motivate you to be persistent.

Deepak Chopra speaks about a "fixity of purpose," which is "holding your attention to the intended outcome with such unbending purpose that you absolutely refuse to allow obstacles" to interfere with your goal.

A striking example of such "attention to an intended outcome" is the creation of the modern state of Israel. In August of 1897, the first Zionist Congress was held in Switzerland, under the leadership of Theodor Herzl,

> *"Ah, but a man's reach should exceed his grasp, or what's a heaven for?"*
>
> – Robert Browning

for the purpose of planning such a state. How absolutely crazy it seemed! Jews were scattered across the world in a condition of powerlessness. Gather them together and have them form a political state? Nonsense. But Herzl believed in his plan and did not consider it nonsense. In fact, he predicted that within 50 years of that Congress there would be a state. And incredibly, almost exactly 50 years later, the modern State of Israel came into being. Herzl had true "fixity of purpose." He stated clearly, "If you will it, it is no dream."

This is the same thing that Colin Powell calls "stick-to-it-ivity." It is what Nathan McCall was demonstrating when he managed to achieve a degree in journalism with honors, while in Norfolk State Prison. It is what Sally Jesse Raphael means when she says, "The only talent is perseverance."

Call it will, or perseverance, or fire within. What we see is that the difference between the dream that succeeds and the dream that does not has less to do with outside factors than with attitude.

The Athenian, Demosthenes, is a classic example of what fierce determination can achieve. As a boy, he had physical infirmities including a tendency to stutter. He lost his father when he was seven and was treated badly by his guardians; he had no formal schooling. Yet, through dedicated effort, he turned himself into one of the greatest orators of the world.

The actor, Chistopher Reeves, is paralyzed from the neck down as the result of a riding accident. No one would have blamed him if he had given up. But he

"There is no failure except in no longer trying. There is no defeat except from within, no really insurmountable barrier save our own inherent weakness of purpose."
—Kin Hubbard

appeared on television many times and even directed a film after becoming paralyzed. Those who work with him are astounded by his positive attitude.

Make a Conscious Decision

At this point, you should be ready to make a conscious decision whether to pursue this dream or not. Consider all the costs, obstacles, and risks, as well as the benefits. Decide if the return on investment is worth it? Evaluate the cost to benefit ratio, the positives and negatives. Visualize the outcome. How will you feel when you have realized the dream? Think in colors, sounds, smells. Think of what can be! Then check your gut reaction. You may decide to go for it, even if the dream causes you to gulp.

Persevere

After you make a conscious decision to pursue the dream, you will have the power to persevere on its behalf. Develop a sense of creative expectancy. Can you see it? When you "just know" your dream can come true, you will be ready to take the actions that will make it happen. When you make an authentic personal commitment to do whatever it takes to bring your dream into reality, your dream becomes a vision. Such commitment leads to follow-through. You are ready to take the next step.

ADDITIONAL RESOURCES:
The Universal Traveler, Don Koberg and Jim Bagnall
The Greatest Risk of All, Walter Anderson

> **Commitment Leads to Courage**
> *Know what you want.*
> *Decide to have it.*

YOUR TURN – TAKE ACTION

Exercise Your Power to Choose

Factors bearing on the decision might include:

Risks	Obstacles	Resources
ridicule	lack of time or energy	connections
alienation	lack of focus	skills
failure	unsympathetic spouse	leadership
success	fear	abilities

Potential solutions	Benefits
college classes	greater self-respect
synergy from strategic alliance	greater self-confidence
mentor	professional pride
get better organized	peace of mind
change attitude	philanthropy
affirmations and visualization	more fun

1. Look closer at the possibility of transforming your dream into a vision. What are the...

    A. Risks?

    _____
    _____
    _____
    _____
    _____
    _____
    _____
    _____

B. Obstacles, real and perceived?

C. Potential solutions to obstacles?

D. Resources, human, financial, and others?

E. Benefits of achieving the dream?

2. What price are you willing to pay?

3. Develop several scenarios describing what might happen in your future. Do some "what if" drills to anticipate your actions.

4. Have you made an authentic, personal commitment?

*A friend may well
be reckoned the
masterpiece
of Nature.*

–Ralph Waldo Emerson

SECTION THREE

Form a Support Team

Chapter 11

Share Your Vision

You have selected a dream, analyzed it and decided to act upon it. Now for the next step, share your vision. Who are those people who will be most affected by your quest? Who has the greatest stake in your success?

You need not walk alone. As John Donne observed over 400 years ago, "No man is an island." The wisdom of his words reverberates soundly in our own time. Whatever your dream, and however strong a commitment you have made to it, it is not likely to become reality if you operate in isolation.

As you look for resources, the first that will come to mind is other people, a mentor surely, but many others, too. Who can you count on to support this bright idea and become involved with you? This means calling upon others to join your effort. The most effective way of doing that is to take them along the path you have already walked.

> *"A sure way for one to lift himself up is by helping lift someone else."*
> – Booker T. Washington

Make a List

Begin with the most important persons in your life who you believe will be supportive. You will be more inclined to see their comments as helpful suggestions, rather than criticisms. At this point, you need encouragement more than help in fine-tuning your ideas. As your belief grows stronger you will be better able to handle opposing opinions.

Think of who must buy into your dream. They may include your spouse or significant other, your immediate family members, your boss, your banker, or other persons who might provide financial backing. Among those you would like to have in agreement with your vision are your mentor and close friends. Start making your list now, while you're still working the first steps of the process.

> *As I was explaining this process to my friend, Maria, she said, "I don't have anyone to share with. I'm single, my parents are older, and my brother certainly doesn't care." We expanded the search to include close friends or a significant other, but there were none. We then looked at what sort of support she might need and found that her dream would require a substantial investment. She would have to convince a banker or financial broker of the value of her ideas. Her dream affected her work situation, so she needed to talk with her boss at some point. It also involved learning new skills. Maria decided to hire a coach.*

First Look for Supportive People

In sharing your vision, first look for compassion and trust. Begin to develop a feeling of inclusiveness. Leave

"A shortcut to becoming a true person: put the right people beside you. The company you keep can work wonders."
–Baltasar Gracián

the "devil's advocates," those bent on finding an opposing view, until later. You may even decide not to tell certain people who will try to dissuade you. That may be a wise decision. At first, your intent is to generate enthusiasm for your ideas.

You are looking for people who have a positive mental attitude, or a predisposition to agree with you. They will be most helpful as you take the first steps toward your desired outcome. These are the people you can call upon when you become discouraged, when things are not going as well as you think they should.

Have you ever felt the power of encouraging other people to take risks, to reach for new heights, to go out on a limb? You assured them that if the risk didn't turn out okay, you would still be there for them after the adventure--success or failure. You were on their side, not laughing or ridiculing, but urging them onward to ever greater heights. We encourage young children, "Come on, you can walk! Come on, take the first step." That's what you are looking for as you share with other people. You are looking for someone to be "on your side."

Break Bread with Them

One of the easiest ways I have found to talk with people is to "break bread" with them. Have lunch, brunch or dinner. Even a cup of tea or coffee will do. When people are munching on something, they tend to relax. Your bright idea turns into another subject of conversation. You are not "on stage."

"Strength is a matter of the made up mind."
–John Beecher

Don't be disappointed if you initially find a lack of enthusiasm for your dream. In some cases, people close to you do not want you to get hurt or feel the disappointment of failure. They are being cautious, protecting you. Remember, it's okay to find another dream if someone you trust has a persuasive argument against what you thought was a great way to go.

As you begin to take action, it is very important to know who to talk with when you are feeling low. You are not yet prepared to hear, "I told you so," or "If only you had listened to me," when things do not go as you expected. Before I learned this lesson, I called the wrong person when I was feeling discouraged. She figuratively held my head under water! I felt much worse after talking with her and was lucky to have someone more positive to talk with soon afterward.

Let Them Help You

Among the people you enroll in your dream will be those who can help you reach it. Allow them to be involved. They will provide energy and "know how" that may help you persevere. Many people find it difficult to accept help. "I can do it better and faster myself." "It takes too long to explain it to other people." "If I accept their help, then I'll owe them something." Remember, no person is an island. No one has all the answers and pay back can take many forms. Find support early in the process and your journey will be more fun and rewarding!

> *Arlon is an avid fisherman. He decided that since he couldn't afford to buy a boat, he would build one in his garage. He immediately realized he'd need to sell his wife on the idea; she agreed,*

but was not enthusiastic. His children didn't think it would last, so they were willing to give up their play space. Arlon bought books and consulted others who had built wooden boats. Soon he was ready. He worked diligently. Then he began receiving unsolicited assistance, such as sections of board for his birthday. This unexpected support resulted from his enthusiasm and demonstrated determination to finish the project.

At last, the inside of the boat was finished and it had to be turned upside down. Though his neighbors jokingly called him "Noah," they gladly helped him flip it over. They knew that in some cases you have to give before you get. They had visions of fishing trips as their reward.

Understand the Law of Reciprocity

What goes around comes around. When people do things that make life easier for you, they may not expect repayment. But at some level, you will take note of their willingness, their assistance, and their unselfishness. You will recall how good that made you feel. You may never have an opportunity to repay those individuals, but you will have opportunities to "pass it on." There will be times when you can help someone else feel a little better. Think of all the talents you have been given and the times others have helped you along the way. Paying back can be a very pleasurable experience.

Ten No-Cost or Low-Cost Ways to Show Appreciation

1. Say "thank you" and tell the person specifically what it is you appreciate and why you appreciate it.

2. Send an e-mail note or an online greeting card.

3. Present a US flag that has flown over the Capitol. It is a unique, reasonably priced item which few people own. A certificate of authenticity is provided in honor of the occasion. Call your congressman's office and ask for it. Flags are available in cotton or nylon and are reasonably priced. If you don't have a local contact, call 202 224-3121 and ask for your congressman or congresswoman by name. When you reach this person's office, ask to purchase a flag.

4. Send a hand-written thank-you note.

5. Present a small certificate.

6. Give a single flower from your garden or flowerpot.

7. Put a candy bar or piece of fruit on his desk, with or without a note. (Be sure the person is not on vacation!)

8. Bake them some cookies. Especially effective when men do this!

9. Say something nice about someone when he or she can overhear you.

10. Place an unexpected phone call to say "hello."

Get Others Excited About Your Vision!

Capture the imagination of those you hope to have in agreement with you. Infuse your message with words that will evoke emotions. An East German physician visited a Toastmasters Club I belonged to at the time the Berlin Wall was being torn down. Someone asked him, "What does it take to bring down a government?" A hush came over the room as we all turned toward him. He began, "It takes a feeling." Pushing his gray suit coat aside with both hands, he clasped his hands to his stomach and said, "When enough people get the same strong feeling inside, nothing can stop them."

Wrap your message in feelings. Share your vision with enthusiasm, conveying conviction and determination. When people see you with "fire in the belly" and "sparkle in your eyes," they'll know you are on the way to getting what you want.

Associates must be convinced of your commitment before they're willing to invest their time and energy to help you. If you're merely going to direct from the sidelines, like a coach, rather than being the quarterback on the playing field, they will probably find another game to play.

Continue to Build

Enrolling others, building alliances, is an on-going process. Even after you feel you have the support you need, continue to search for others you might want to enroll. Sharpen your networking skills. Draw on those

> *"Our chief want in life is somebody who shall make us do what we can."*
> —Ralph Waldo Emerson

who are already on your team and use their commitment and enthusiasm to expand your contacts. The bandwagon effect is very powerful.

Keep in Touch

After people buy into your vision, they will want to know about your progress. Find a way to let them know.

- Develop a mailing list of your support team.

- Use postcards to write notes.

- Send an e-mail update.

- Develop a brief newsletter and send it on a regular basis.

- Occasionally telephone key players. They can help keep your enthusiasm at a high level.

Develop a Support Team
Share your dream with supportive people first.
Ask for what you want.
Learn from others.

Chapter 12

Tell It Like It Is

Having completed the first steps in this process, you are ready to "let the world know!" It is time to "sell" your vision to others you can count on for compassion and trust. Don't expect everyone to hop on board the first time you mention your vision. Be prepared to work at it, until people are convinced and they can begin to see what you have already seen. Repetition is the cadence of the universe. Potential members of your team may have to hear what you are planning many times before they understand and are convinced.

Talk in a way that attracts and excites people. The more you talk about your vision, the clearer and more real it will become to you. As you share your vision with others, they will develop a feeling of inclusion even though, at first, they may only watch what you do. Demonstrate your commitment. Make it easy for others to buy into your ideas, but don't be discouraged if they are slow to do so.

Provide Solid Information

Study your topic and be certain you know all you need to know to get started. What is it you are hoping to do? Think of the outcome, the result of your endeavor.

Think how it will make you feel to have succeeded. Paint verbal pictures for your listeners. Descriptions affecting our senses make a greater impact. Use colors, sounds, smells and feelings to describe your ideas.

Face the Fear

Having to articulate what you've been thinking to yourself may cause you to stop in your tracks! "No way," you say. "They'll ask questions I can't answer. They may remind me that I've never done anything like this before. I won't be able to explain it well enough."

Such thoughts are just the first challenges on your journey to achievement. Overcoming these challenges will strengthen you as you proceed in the face of this fear. Consider it part of paying up front for that which you will have in the end.

Breaking bread together usually puts people at greater ease. If you are having a cup of coffee or lunch with a friend and talking about your dream, you are more likely to be relaxed. If that opportunity is not available to you, think of your discussion as an adventure. It's like going into uncharted territory, exploring and discovering new ideas. It can be great fun!

Don't wait for others to buy in. Get moving. People are waiting to see you do something. When you get into action, they will know you are serious.

> *"Fear makes men ready to believe the worst."*
> –Quintus Curtius Rufus

Practice These Techniques

- Calm yourself by taking deep breaths.

- Formulate your thoughts into sentences and write out an outline so it makes sense to you.

- Think about the persons to whom you will be

speaking. What do you know about them? What is likely to be their reaction? Prepare to respond.

- Do not resort to being coy or manipulative.

- Focus on mental images of the successful outcome you have set out to accomplish.

Communicate Clearly

Speak with conviction and enthusiasm. Show that you've "done your homework." Think in terms of who, what, where, when and how.

- What is your vision; what are you trying to accomplish?

- Why do you want it?

- What are the benefits and who benefits? What do you want from the individual to whom you are talking? It may be only moral support.

- Who is involved or may be required to contribute something toward your vision?

- How do you plan to get the outcome you want? You may have only very sketchy plans at first. That's okay, you've just begun. As you talk with more people who are supportive and

"Assumptions are the termites of relationships."
                                          –Henry Winkler

as you think more about your vision, a course of action will become clearer. The important thing is to be prepared to take the first step without knowing every step that must be taken.

- When do you think the vision will be realized?

- What is your timeline–five years? ten years? longer?

- Where will this activity take place? Do you plan to relocate, or can your vision be accomplished where you are today?

Acknowledge Support and Involvement

The greater the involvement of other persons, the more important it is that you listen to their ideas and possibly modify your thinking to get their agreement. Their contributions might be money, time, energy, or other resources. Unless you consider their comments, you run the risk of losing their support.

Sandy once dreamed of an expensive home and set a goal to have it. Her husband was not aware of this. Sandy worked hard to improve their financial situation. She later discovered that her husband could not be persuaded to agree with her dream. He was not interested in moving from their modest home. Eventually the couple divorced.

> *"It's what you learn after you know it all that counts."*
> —Anonymous

Think back to your values and the relationships you

cherish. Be sure to share your vision with the people who mean the most to you. Be prepared to modify or change your vision if the relationship is threatened.

Let Them Know You Know the Challenges

Tell about the potential obstacles and risks. Show that you have considered them and thought of possible solutions. This will indicate that you are serious and intend to work toward a successful outcome, in spite of the challenges.

Be wary. People tend to be judgmental. Do not let negative thinkers throw you off course. Follow your own good judgment. It is okay to ask others if they can think of something you may have overlooked. Make them feel important.

When You Face Ridicule

Sometimes people thoughtlessly laugh at our ideas. When you get ridicule in response, don't feel embarrassed. Quietly take a deep breath. You might say, "What I hear you saying is that you don't believe I can do this. I can understand why you might think that way and I want to assure you that I have thought this through. I have considered the obstacles and risks and looked for potential solutions. It won't happen overnight, but I'm committed to working it out over time. I'm open to your suggestions. Your input is valuable to me."

> *"Nothing great in the world has ever been accomplished without passion."*
>
> –Hegel

If you are unsure of your communication skills, join a Toastmasters Club. You will find compassion and empathy as well as an opportunity to practice your communication skills. Call 1 800 9WESPEAK for information on the club nearest you or look them up on the Internet at www.toastmasters.com.

Be Enthusiastic, Even Passionate About Your Vision

Show your excitement; it is contagious and conveys the depth of your own involvement. Remember, it is the fire inside of you that is going to light sparks in others.

When people see the sparkle in your eyes, and hear the excitement in your voice, they will know that you are on the way to extraordinary achievement. More importantly, they will want to go with you!

Speak Persuasively
Think before you speak.
Be concise, don't ramble.
Speak with conviction and feeling.

Chapter 13

Let Them Talk

Be prepared to listen, as well as to speak. As Edgar W. Howe reminds us, "No one would listen to you talk if they didn't know it was their turn next."

Thus, in the process of sharing your vision, you must allow others to help shape it. Show that your mind can be changed if someone can convince you it's the right way to go. If you are receptive to what others say, you will learn a good deal that is worthwhile.

Pay Attention

By listening, you will be setting a tone that tells others that what they say has value. You will be actively demonstrating that, even in the early planning stages, they can make a difference.

At the same time, you do not want to appear to be asking for approval, unless of course, you need it. A tactful response to their ideas may be, "Thank you for that suggestion. It will help flesh out my ideas in that area," or "Your comments give me another perspective on that issue. I will consider them."

The Desiderata, found in old St. Paul's Church in Baltimore, MD, dated 1692, advises us to listen to others, "even the dull and ignorant; they too have their story."

Become a More Effective Listener

Effective listening is an art. It requires you to:

- Respect others and acknowledge their perceptions as valuable.

- Reevaluate your assumptions and biases, and work to eliminate your stereotypes.

- Pay attention to what is said. Do not permit yourself to be distracted.

- Take notes. Jot down words that will jog your memory for follow-up actions.

- Be attentive to what is not said, but don't jump to conclusions prematurely. Is the speaker trying not to offend you and sidestepping a question? Check out your hunch by verifying it with the speaker.

- Ask questions and paraphrase for fuller understanding.

- Use your body language in a positive way. Make eye contact. Nod appropriately and appreciatively. Lean forward.

- Avoid being defensive about your ideas.

- Avoid signs of restlessness while listening, such as tapping a pencil.

"You cannot teach a man anything; you can only help him to find it within himself."
–Galileo

Make Them Feel Important

Some time ago, I was interviewing a very important person for another book I was writing. The phone rang as he was speaking and he courteously asked if I'd mind if he answered it. He had asked his secretary to hold his calls, but there was one important matter he needed to tend to and this must be it. Of course, I didn't mind. What amazed me was that when he returned to our conversation, he picked up exactly at the point we'd been interrupted, practically in mid-sentence. Had I not been taking notes, I would have been less prepared to pick up listening where he'd left off. He made me feel important because, though he needed to take the phone call, he did not lose sight of our conversation. This is a skill worth imitating.

> **Powerful Listening**
> Screen out distractions.
> Turn off the TV.
> Ask questions to get a better understanding.
> Give feedback to be sure you get the intent of a message.

ADDITIONAL RESOURCES:
52 Ways to Reconnect, Follow-Up and Stay in Touch, Anne Baber and Lynne Waymon
Talking from 9 to 5, Deborah Tannen
101 ways to Improve Your Communication Skills Instantly, Jo Condrill and Bennie Bough, Ph.D.

Chapter 14

Lessons Harry Taught Me

"I think you're nuts!" Harry whispered under his breath, but I heard and was aghast! This was a Leadership Breakfast, and I was the leader talking to the group of volunteers seated around the tables. I was trying to sell them on stretching for a higher goal than they thought possible. Filled with enthusiasm, I was trying to convince them that they were capable of much more than we had accomplished in the past. The challenge was to become champions. I worked for the "Be All You Can Be" Army and firmly believed in their motto.

The upper echelon of the leadership group had already bought into the idea of reaching a higher goal. Harry was Treasurer; surely he knew. Why did he raise an objection now? Apparently, he was not sold!

My mind raced as I continued the speech. How do I address Harry's comment? How will it affect the others who heard it? What must I do to regain the confidence of those who had bought in earlier?

An inspiration came to me as I continued speaking. Everyone does not have to go along with the idea, at first, for it to be worthy of action. Those who do can begin to take steps to bring it into reality. As their determination is seen and progress is made, others will find it easier to become convinced of the merit of the idea. It's like pulling a toboggan uphill in the snow. No one wants to have to do the work, but everyone wants to pile on when the toboggan is set for the downhill run. It's that bandwagon effect again.

I reassured the group at the Leadership Breakfast that it was okay if they didn't yet believe we could reach our goal. They only needed to think of their own personal goals for the time being. When the rest of us began to make strides toward our objective, it would be easier for them to buy in. And, so we began. In the end, we exceeded our goal. We had expanded our membership 18% and excelled in the education program.

Harry taught me a valuable lesson that day. We can't wait for everyone to buy into our ideas. If we are convinced and committed, we must take action right away. There will always be negative thinkers and "devil's advocates" who will tell us it can't be done. If we have carefully considered our course of action, looked at the potential obstacles and risks, and then made a conscious decision to take action, we will not easily be swayed by those who do not believe.

Some years after this incident, Harry gave me permission to tell it publicly. But, he added, "You didn't hear the rest of my comment. I said, 'You just might do it.' " Another lesson: listen harder!

10 Keys to Communicating Your Vision

1. Carefully select the people with whom you want to share your vision.

2. Clearly explain the vision to them, one at a time, or in very small groups.

3. Tell them what you think their role will be, e.g. encourager, participant, advisor.

4. Let your enthusiasm show. Capture their imagination!

5. Let them know that you know there will be obstacles and that you have considered potential solutions.

6. Allow them to ask questions and answer them honestly.

7. Be willing to modify ideas to accommodate some of their ideas if they are to be a participant in your vision.

8. Ask for input. Then, listen with an open mind to what others have to say.

9. Be prepared for negative responses. This is the first test of your resolve.

10. Be grateful. Demonstrate your commitment.

YOUR TURN–TAKE ACTION

Develop a Support Team

1. Who do you need to have in agreement with you?

    Family members:

    _____
    _____
    _____
    _____
    _____
    _____
    _____
    _____
    _____
    _____
    _____

    Friends and Associates:

    _____
    _____
    _____
    _____
    _____
    _____
    _____
    _____
    _____

Boss:

2. What potential resources can you identify?

3. What affiliations do you need to cultivate?

Checklist for Selling Your Ideas

__ Involve people who have a stake in your decisions, as well as those who can support your ideas.

__ Convey facts and feelings.

__ Communicate vision, beliefs, and benefits.

__ Communicate clearly with conviction and enthusiasm.

Who–What–Where–Why–When–How

__ Paint mental pictures.

__ Listen. Dean Rusk said one of the best ways to persuade others is with your ears, by listening.

__ Be open to input from people you wish to enroll.

__ Consider their opinions. Let them know you value their ideas, whether you use them or not.

__ Know that there will be obstacles, but demonstrate your commitment to achieving your vision.

__ Talk about what's in it for them.

*A single conversation
across the table
with a wise man
is worth
a month's study
of books.*

–Chinese Proverb

SECTION FOUR
Strategic Alliances

Chapter 15

Forming a Strategic Alliance

As you begin to make the list of your support team, consider the benefits of forming a strategic alliance based on the "Master Mind" concept of Napoleon Hill. Such alliances have been used by the most successful and the wealthiest people in the world.

A "Master Mind" group is different from a circle of friends. This is a specially selected group that can work together in absolute harmony to achieve their goals.

While these people work in harmony, they may be very different from each other. The common element is that each draws something from the others, and each contributes freely to the others. It is the focusing of each mind on a common issue that triggers thoughts not readily available to one mind. Those in the group draw upon their unique experiences and specialized knowledge to help each other. We have seen that the dynamic spirit, and the results of many minds concentrating on a single point in this manner, provides a power over and above the sum total of each of the individual minds. It is as though an invisible force joins the group and provides additional insight.

Study the Concept

The "Master Mind" concept was used by Andrew Carnegie, the great steel maker, early in the twentieth century. It was studied and revealed by Napoleon Hill. I first learned of this concept when I read Hill's book,

Think and Grow Rich. Henry Ford is known to have used this concept. He was inventive, innovative, and highly successful. His associates included Thomas A. Edison, Harvey Firestone, John Burroughs, and Luther Burbank, all creative thinkers with "can do" attitudes.

A Two-Person Alliance

Before forming an alliance with these people, however, Ford's wife was his confidant and supporter. It was she who encouraged him to keep trying. When bankers were not willing to loan them money so Henry could continue his experiments, Mrs. Ford suggested that they use money they were saving to buy a house as collateral. With the money they received in the loan, Mr. Ford was able to continue his work and eventually achieved the vision they both believed was possible.

Have you seen this principle working in your life? I have used it with amazing results. First, to advance my career and later, to lead a group of volunteers to achieve remarkable things. Find out what others have said about their experiences in "Master Mind" groups at the end of this section.

My Not So Secret Formula

There is no magic formula for this special group. However, it is sometimes easier to understand a concept by using symbols.

$$P_{(p+n)} (O+C+B+PA) (HDA) = ESA$$

$P_{(p+n)}$	= Two or more persons
O	= Objective or purpose
C	= Contribution
B	= Benefit
PA	= Positive Attitude
H	= Harmony
D	= Determination
A	= Action
ESA	= Effective Strategic Alliance

Two or more persons multiplied by the sum of their objectives or purposes plus contributions and benefits, plus a positive mental attitude, multiplied by the harmony, determination and actions of the group, equal an effective strategic alliance based on the "Master Mind" concept.

Alliance in Action

$P_{(p+n)}$ — Two or more persons come together for their mutual benefit. The number of people in the group may vary. A couple can form an alliance based on the "Master Mind" concept. An uneven number of people, such as 3, 5, or 7 are said to work better than an even number. I know of no study which would bear this out, however. The number of participants is not as important as is their ability to work in harmony with all the other participants. The larger the group, the harder it may be to accomplish harmony on a continuous basis.

Objective Participants must have specific purposes for belonging. The group may focus on individual objectives or a group objective. A person may belong to more than one group at the same time.

Contribution Each person must have something to contribute to others in the group, a specific talent, leads, or specialized knowledge such as marketing or organizational skills. One member I know presents tips, or leads, at each meeting. This is her gift to the group. Your contribution could be as basic as good will and encouraging words.

Benefit Each person must gain something by participating in the group. That gain will not always be material. It may be increased self-confidence or "know how." Ultimately, it may be the realization of a dream.

Positive Attitude To be effective, members of the group must have a positive expectation of good results from their participation. This is not to suggest that there will not be challenges or frustrations. A positive mental attitude means that the individuals are predisposed to view things in a positive frame of mind. Negative thinkers focus on why ideas will not work, rather than on trying to find ways to make them work. People with PA also acknowledge that sometimes an idea is simply not worth pursuing. To ignore the facts is foolhardy. There is a fine line between persistently moving toward one's vision and being able to alter one's course when necessary. The challenge is in seeing the "big picture," relationships of various facets of our lives, being able to see the obstacles, and recognizing when it is prudent to pull back and reevaluate the situation.

Harmony For a like-minded alliance to survive, there must be a high level of trust and respect among the participants. When there is goodwill and harmony, everyone gains. When envy and resentment enter in, harmony fades.

Determination Results do not happen overnight. The alliance is not a quick-fix solution. Remaining focused on the objective and persisting in the face of challenges are key elements of the process.

Action Group participation is stimulating, but the group will not be successful without individual action outside the group. Members should discuss progress from time to time and, by mutual agreement, hold each other accountable for taking action. This encourages celebrating each other's successes and strengthens bonds within the group.

Not everyone you enroll in your vision will be in your strategic alliance. The phenomenon of the "Master Mind" concept is, in part, cumulative wisdom and knowledge. Many persons know more, have experienced more, have a greater variety of perceptions, than any single individual has. When each can draw upon the collective mind power of the group, he or she is greatly strengthened. Add to this the spiritual dimension, or the force of synergism, and you see the added value of a strategic alliance using the "Master Mind" concept.

Strategic Alliances
Regular access to like-minded individuals
Trusting relationships
Shared knowledge
Spirit of harmony

Chapter 16

Take the Initiative

While forming a strategic alliance may sound complicated, think of it this way: Each must see, "What's in it for me?" Group members must get enough satisfaction to keep them working in harmony. The people in the group usually do not have the same goal. Several people are working on individual goals that do not affect the others. Yet, all contribute ideas and draw energy from the others.

Too often we seek out people who are just like us. We want people who think like we do, who do what we do. We are comfortable with these people and can usually expect them to agree with us. When forming a strategic alliance, you need people who are not like you.

Why Form Such a Group?

What is a logical objective for you to form a group based on the "Master Mind" concept? Specialized knowledge. Benefit from the experience and skills of the group. Maybe your vision is to become a famous stand-up comic. You don't have any contacts in that field and are not sure what steps to take, other than to become funny. You need help to stimulate your thinking, and you need a larger network to help you discover resources. You may be seeking financial assistance and encouragement, as well as specialized knowledge.

Bev Williams, founder of the Home-Based Business Association, helped organize a "Master Mind" group. Bev said, "As a home-based business owner, I missed the camaraderie of co-workers, brainstorming ideas, and the 'push' of having others know my plans and holding me accountable for what I said I would do. I missed sharing the joy of my accomplishments with others who understood what I was trying to accomplish." As a professional speaker, she wanted to both give and get support and information from other speakers. "The Master Mind group I helped form still does all those things for me," Bev says.

A major breakthrough came as Bev was struggling with the idea of writing a book about her knowledge of and experiences with home-based businesses. "The thought of writing it all down was overwhelming. I had been procrastinating for years!" Her "Master Mind" associates tried brainstorming and suggesting resources and helpful hints, but she was still fighting the process. "It came to me one day that I didn't have to write a book to get my information to market – I could produce an audio tape with the information. No one else had done a tape for the industry and yet, audio tapes are very popular. With the help of my group, I found the resources and help I needed. Working with the group helped strengthen my self-confidence and stimulated my creative imagination." As a result, she produced a tape with valuable information that will help anyone trying to form a profitable home-based business, and Bev will realize a small profit at the same time.

Know Whom to Select

After you have figured out a purpose, list people you know who have the knowledge and skills you seek. You are looking for people who are action oriented, have a reasonably high energy level, and will follow-through on commitments. Attending meetings will take away some of their already scarce leisure time, so show your appreciation if they decide to join you.

If there is no one you know who has the qualities you seek, ask yourself, "Whom do I know who might know a person with these qualities?" Ask yourself if this is someone you can trust. Will this person be discreet and keep confidences? Can you build a trusting relationship with that person? Would you be willing to meet with him or her on a regular basis in a spirit of confidence? This should be the kind of person who wishes you well.

For example, if you want to become a stand-up comic, whom do you know in the field of comedy? Whom do you know who can introduce you to someone successful in that field? Do you know people in related arts or in training? Find people who are action oriented and share your values. It will be of no benefit to you if these people only talk about people they know. You want them to take action and facilitate an introduction.

Lead the Group

Leadership of the group initially rests with the person forming the group. His or her responsibility is to

> "A mind stretched by a new idea never returns to its original dimension."
> —James Lincoln

set the meeting time and place until the group is formed and makes its own decision. Leadership of meetings may then rotate. For instance, one person leads the session for a month; then the next month, someone else is the leader. There are no records kept except each individual's private notes. With an established process and ground rules, there is no need for an elected or designated leader. When a spokesperson is needed, the person with the longest standing in the group is designated.

Form Ground Rules

Once you have decided to form a group, think of how the group will operate. Ground rules provide some structure. Is everyone expected to attend all meetings? Where and when will the group meet? Who will lead the meetings? Leadership might rotate or rest in one individual. Do members agree to be accountable to each other for taking actions they say they will? Are there other expectations of members? How will those who do not abide by the ground rules be treated?

Decide on Meetings

Decide how often and in what manner you should meet. Some groups meet weekly, others twice a month. Some meet face-to-face; others use conference calls. It depends on your circumstances. I prefer to meet face-

> *"Everything is in the mind. That's where it all starts. Knowing what you want is the first step toward getting it."*
>
> —Mae West

to-face. Distances may make that difficult for you. The important things are that a bond is formed, that there is mutual trust and a sense of well being, and that you are willing to be vulnerable and ask for help.

How Long Does the Group Stay Together?

How long does membership in a group last? It depends on your purpose. You may collectively determine at the outset how long the group will exist. I belonged to one such group and the results were very much worthwhile. On the other hand, it may be open-ended with members coming and going periodically over time. While this would change the dynamics of the group, it is sometimes best for the group.

Set the Agenda

Do you have an established agenda for each meeting? Who decides what you talk about? We think of near term goals at most of the meetings, goals that can be met within the year. Sometimes we need brainstorming to help stimulate our creative thinking. Sometimes we let others know what we would like to discuss, but not routinely. With a one to two hour meeting, we take about 20 minutes each to discuss our topic. Often, we find ideas we can apply to our situation while we are discussing someone else's topic. We also want to come prepared to give something to the group. That may be a tip, a connection in the form of a phone number or address, or just a word of encouragement.

> *"Knowledge is power."*
> —Sir Francis Bacon

Listening to other people talk about their dreams or projects allows us to pick up bits of information. We might not have been interested in those topics before we began meeting. These groups expand our thinking.

Make the Tough Decisions

Sometimes members become lackadaisical. They lose sight of why they are in the group. Perhaps they become envious, or new members change the dynamics of the group and it is just not working.

When this happens and you find that you are not getting the benefits you want from the group, it is best to terminate your membership. You may simply need to back off and center yourself again. You may want to form a different group with different skills and specialized knowledge. It is best to leave with no ill will, no hurt feelings.

What if the person who should leave does not see it that way? Someone in the group must take the initiative and talk with that person privately and suggest that he or she find another group. It is in the best interest of all concerned.

Try It

While these groups can be extremely beneficial, they are not essential to your success. Not all groups are "Master Mind" groups. Not everyone needs a "Master Mind" group. The power of such a group is drawn from the mix of specialized knowledge which is freely shared in a spirit of harmony. If at all possible, try one and evaluate the results.

> **Alliances in Action**
> *Select wisely.*
> *Meet regularly.*
> *Share openly.*

ADDITIONAL RESOURCES:
Think and Grow Rich, Napoleon Hill
The Science of Personal Achievement, Napoleon Hill

Chapter 17

How an Effective Strategic Alliance Worked for Me

In 1991, I was elected to lead a 3,000 member volunteer organization, District 27, Toastmasters International. The group's purpose is to enhance communication and leadership skills. About ten months prior to assuming my new responsibility, I assembled a group of people who had held that position at some time in the past. The people selected had been supportive of my efforts in the past and I trusted them. Surely we could work in harmony. Our group's purpose was to help me become the best governor I could be and to discover what was possible for the District to achieve that year.

Among those selected were Pauline Shirley, who had led her District in Texas to a #1 ranking; Mike Wardinski, who had been my mentor a few years earlier; and Bennie Bough, who became my co-author a few years later. We met in my living room monthly. We brainstormed, shared experiences, and explored possibilities. They pointed out expectations of the people I would be leading and discussed organizational policies. They challenged me to set goals and formulate strategies to attain them. Always helpful, they never ridiculed my ideas.

However, they did not go along with all my ideas. As I was developing my theme for the year, the group was not enthusiastic about any of my suggestions. I selected the one I liked best, "Give It All You've Got!" After mulling it over some more, the group accepted it and even suggested a rousing response, "Yes!" My year was launched.

The group then transformed itself into a Board of Advisors, trusted agents I could call upon for guidance. Out of this early effort, grew the enthusiasm and know-how that propelled us to rank #1 in Toastmasters International based on organizational growth and an excellent educational program.

Survey responses

This informal survey was conducted in October 1998, in the Washington, DC, area. All responders were participants in groups using the Master Mind principles of Napoleon Hill as their model. The following are selected anonymous responses that demonstrate the positive impact of this model.

Why do you belong to a "Master Mind" group?

"It's a powerful way to get ideas and support from other like-minded individuals. As Napoleon Hill said, the importance of the master mind concept is the synergy of the group. It's like adding an additional person to the group."

"To contribute and to receive the benefits of having a number of minds focusing on the concerns and problems I experience in working toward my vision."

"Because I want to support and help others like me and gain support and help for my endeavors, too. I learn important insights and gain advice I would never learn otherwise, and hope I give that same kind of value in return."

"The group helps you remove your limitations, in your thinking and in your goals for yourself. The members have helped me stretch my comfort zone and I hope I've helped them stretch their own."

What do you gain from belonging to such a group?

"The group dynamics of a supportive team, that is support with a capital "S." I've seen myself reach some goals which absolutely astound me!"

"It is invaluable because it keeps me focused, on track and committed to excellence. I think it is important to have members we each trust implicitly, on whom we can depend for support and who we like personally as friends. I'm looking forward to being part of this productive group for years to come."

"ACTION and more personalized attention. When we become a part of a master mind group, we have to be an active participant. We are more observant of our own commitment and the commitment of the participants. It gives us an opportunity to provide ideas and answers to others and of course, get ideas and answers to our own challenges. The main benefit of a MMG is the personal interaction of each member of the group and the strong support for each other."

"Safety, trust. Other members don't laugh at your ideas and won't be hurt by honest comments on their ideas because they know you care about them."

"The positive results of not just shortening the learning curve, but the energy and imagination of others in the group have enhanced my efforts."

"We are diverse enough to really see things from totally different points of view. Most groups have so much in common that there seldom are any fresh looks at any topic of discussion."

"It's great to know when you arrive at the top of the mountain that friends will be there with you!"

What do you contribute to the group?

"First respect of others. Also sharing my experiences, trials and struggles."

"A positive 'can do' attitude and a spiritual lean to everything."

"I hope my insights, knowledge and enthusiasm helps others gain insight into different ways they can achieve their goals, maybe think of different ways to do things - alternatives they might not have thought of themselves. I also hope my support and encouragement keeps them on track!!!!!"

"My contributions are based upon my observations, experience, judgment, and my wish for success of each member."

Specific results?

"Tom's analytical nature has caused me to focus on self-imposed limitations that I was blinded to."

"Forcing me to take action on my goals. It's like losing face. If I don't work toward them I feel like I'm letting the others, and myself, down."

YOUR TURN — TAKE ACTION

Apply the Master Mind Concept

1. Why would you want to join or form a Strategic Alliance?

2. What could you contribute to such a group? Think of specialized knowledge and skills you have.

3. What skills, knowledge, or abilities would you look for in other group members?

4. Whom do you know that you would want in your group?

The world stands aside to let pass the person who knows whither he is going.

–Ordway Tead

SECTION FIVE

Plan and Implement

Chapter 18

Make It Happen

Does your vision have the power to stir up emotions and touch your soul? Does it generate feelings that lead to action?

Envision Your Desired Outcome

After you have formulated your vision and deliberately decided to go for it, you need to develop a strategy. Look at the big picture. What is the dream you have committed to, the outcome you are willing to work toward? See it in your mind. Visualize it. Try to use all your senses; add scents, taste, and sounds. Imagine how it will make you feel when you have finally achieved this vision.

As an aspiring stand-up comic, your vision may be something like the following:

> There you are on center stage with the microphone cradled between your palms. The hot lights are so bright you are perspiring. The audience is laughing out loud, "rolling in the aisles." You are beaming as the TV cameras are panning the full house. The thrill of success washes over you.

Develop a Strategy

It is not necessary to know, at the beginning, everything that will need to be done. You have an outcome in mind. You have analyzed it, looked at obstacles and possibilities for overcoming those obstacles. You have identified resources you may call on.

Develop an idea of how you can get from where you are to where you want to be. Play with it in your mind for a few days. Think of what you will have to do. Who do you need to assist you? Look for things that are building blocks to other objectives.

For example, you can see yourself as the Chief Financial Officer of the corporation where you now work. You like the management, you are in sync with the mission, and you feel you have a chance to achieve your personal vision there. You realize that you don't have the necessary education, credentials, or experience to be the CFO today. So you begin to develop a strategy to attain that position:

> Get the education.
>
> Get the credentials, and in the meantime, move up in the organization to gain the necessary experience.
>
> Keep options open if career progression is slow within the corporation. Lateral moves may be necessary and provide experience that would be helpful.
>
> See yourself already in possession of your desired outcome. Ah, that magnificent office in the corner with the huge desk, oak furniture, and plush carpets

Plan and Implement

> *"Destiny is not a matter of chance, it is a matter of choice; it is not a thing to be waited for, it is a thing to be achieved."*
> —William Jennings Bryan

The contact with the CEO, the Chairman of the Board, your administrative staff! How sweet it is!

Identify the critical success factors. What must be done to ensure success and preclude failure? Study the job requirements. List factors you can identify. Broaden your scope to include all facets of your life, such as, physical activities, involvement with church and community activities, and hobbies.

Chart Your Course
*Start where you are.
Look ahead.
Develop a strategy.*

Chapter 19

Develop an Action Plan

The next step is a tactical one. Break the strategy into pieces that can be accomplished. These pieces may be called goals. There are many methods of goal setting. Many of us are put off by extensive details and formulas. However, some plan must be committed to writing, so that your target is fixed and you can review it from time to time.

This plan does not need to be elaborate or time consuming. It does require some thought. With the outcome in mind, begin by working backward to list major events. In our example of becoming CFO, your list might look something like this:

- Get selected for the CFO position
- Become a Certified Public Accountant
- Get the requisite experience
- Gain visibility within the company
- Get an MBA, and maybe even get a law degree
- Get a degree in accounting

Remember, you are working backward here.

You may even want to add other items such as:

- Maintain physical activity routine

Volunteer to help in civic groups or youth activities, such as Scouting.

Take vacations

These activities will indicate that you maintain some balance in your life. Your involvement in extracurricular activities will provide opportunities to meet people you might not meet in the regular work environment.

Make a List of Known Activities

List everything you can think of that will have to be done to reach each of these major goals. This list will be much longer than the first list. You might organize it using the events as headings. For instance, you might list under the heading of:

GET A DEGREE IN ACCOUNTING:

> Talk with someone in Human Resources, or Management. See if the company will pay for any courses or provide the time and opportunity to attend classes, if necessary.
>
> Get the college catalog.
>
> Talk with a counselor to set up a program. What are the required courses, and when are they offered? Can any of your work experience count for college credit to shorten the classroom time?

> *"Fortune favors the audacious."*
> —Desiderius Erasmus

Develop Family Support

Talk with your spouse, if any, about this new outside activity to gain support. What will it take in class and study time? What will you and the family gain from this activity?

What if there is resistance? You need a contingency plan. If your spouse refuses to cooperate, then here are some alternatives:

1. Attend classes during work hours

2. Take correspondence courses

3. Find courses on the Internet for credit

4. Delay start of courses

At this point, you are trying to better define what needs to be done and when. If there are any shortcuts, now is the time to discover them! You won't know everything that will need to be done. That's okay. You do need to find the first step and take it. Your list will change and grow as you learn more.

Ask for Help

Learn from others who have done what you intend to do. Get the biography or resume of the current CFO. Someone in the administrative or human resources section probably has it. Look at the path this person

> *"The great thing in the world is not so much where we stand, as in what direction we are moving."*
>
> —Oliver Wendell Holmes

took. If feasible, get an appointment and talk with him or her about career paths. Let this person know about your dream, and you may acquire a new mentor, as a result.

Use discretion in discussing your ultimate goal with others, though. Tell them only as much as necessary unless they are trusted confidants who will be supportive.

Refine Your List

After you do some information gathering, make a list of everything you now know will need to be done to reach your final objective. You will find that some things can be grouped together and may even be sequential. That is, you must do one thing before you can do the next. For instance, you want to take some courses right now leading to an accounting degree. However, you are a single parent with no extra money. Before you can take courses, you must find someone to care for the children. The first step might be finding the additional funds to hire someone to take care of the children. Possible solutions might include trading childcare with someone else, or finding a supportive relative or friend who will volunteer to provide the care for awhile without charge.

funds + childcare + classes = degree

When you have listed everything you can think of, prioritize the steps you must take, one at a time.

For those extraneous steps which do not depend on the completion of other steps and may be done at any time, use "Grandma's Law." Simply make a list of these steps, putting the ones you like to do most at the top and the ones you like to do least at the bottom. Then, begin working from the bottom of the list. Remember, Grandma always said you have to eat the vegetables first, then you can have dessert! You'll have more energy to tackle the tough ones you don't like at the beginning, while your enthusiasm is still very high. Otherwise, there might be the human tendency to avoid the less desirable items.

> "Remember, when opportunity knocks, it doesn't know you've had a bad day; greet it with a smile."
>
> –Jim Blasingame

Develop a Time Line

Once you know what must be done, you need to know when it needs to be done. Begin to develop milestones. Timing can be crucial in some areas. For instance, some classes, which are necessary for your degree, may be offered only every other semester. You need to know those things early enough to put them in your time line at the appropriate place. To become CFO within fifteen years, you will need to get that accounting degree within six years, add three years to get the MBA, and one year to pass the CPA exam. You are a part-time student, remember! Build in some fluff; give yourself a buffer in case something does not work out according to plan. This can eliminate major stress at critical junctures in your journey. After you become CPA, you can go back and get that law degree. Meanwhile, you are continuing to gain progressively higher levels of experience. Set deadlines for certain activities and, realize what missing them will cost.

> "We are what we repeatedly do. Excellence,
> then, is not an act, but a habit."
> —Aristotle

You may find yourself anywhere along this time line. If you already have an MBA and your desire is to be CFO, your timeline will be considerably shorter than someone who has a degree in social work, or no degree at all.

Focus on Essentials

"Don't sweat the small stuff," the saying goes. Yet, sometimes it is very hard to discover the difference between what is "small stuff" and what is important. While this is not easy, it is essential to achieving the desired outcome. It is too easy to expend enormous energy on something that is not in line with the desired outcome. This is especially true if you have not taken time to think. When you know what you want, and you intend to get it, more of your energy will be spent on that objective.

There will be times when you want to pull back and take time off. It is important that you do so. Even a battering ram must be pulled back, only to be thrust forward again with renewed vigor to achieve its results.

As you are planning, keep in mind your basic values. Factor in time for yourself, time for your family, as well as for your spiritual needs. Take care of your body. All the achievement in the world is not worth ruining your health. There will be times when you seem out of

> "A genius is a person who aims at something
> no one else can see and hits it."
> —Ervin Glaspy

balance while striving for a lofty goal. That is okay, if you know it is only for a period of time. Then you can bring your life more into balance.

Encourage the Heart

Think of small rewards to attach to the goals or activities that must be accomplished. Put them into your plan. Take time along the way to relax and acknowledge small successes, yours, as well as others who help you.

Take Time to Plan
Reduce the big picture to manageable pieces.
Set deadlines.

Chapter 20

Visualize Don't Fantasize

The key to reaching your goal, of achieving your vision, is belief. Dr. Norman Vincent Peale said the first thing is to get your consciousness soaked with faith. William James agrees that the most important thing, at the beginning of any enterprise, is belief.

Do you believe you either have or can acquire the things necessary to attain your dream? If not, that belief must be developed before you can have what you want. You've probably heard the cliché, "seeing is believing." But the truth is you've got to believe it to see it. Soak your consciousness in faith. It has been said that we become what we think about most of the time.

Create a Goal Poster

I discovered goal posters some years ago when I was trying to begin a new career. It is a simple technique to keep the goal visually in front of us.

The object is to group several visual representations of what you want where you can see them several times a day. Look for images or symbols that represent what you want. Use as many of your senses as possible. Can you smell it—the leather interior of a new car? The fresh mown grass outside your new home? The salt air outside your cabin window? Can you taste it, touch it, see it? Hear the waves massaging the beach? Get clip art from the Internet, cut out photographs from magazines, draw your own pictures. Group them on your computer, or get construction paper and tape them onto it, as I did. Have your collection where you can look at it several times during the day.

You must develop belief—in yourself, that you can reach your goal, and belief that you deserve to reach your goal.

Begin to think how things will be when you reach your goal. Jonathan Swift spoke of "the art of seeing things invisible." Norman Vincent Peale called it "imaging." Eastern thinkers speak of "visualization." Whatever the label, it is a powerful process. It requires you to move beyond merely thinking about what you would like to accomplish, and to picture it vividly. It is the way to find the answers to what you believe you might want to become or achieve.

- Find a peaceful place to be, away from distractions.

- Try to detach yourself from concerns with the mundane details of life.

- Turn down the constant chattering that takes place in your mind.

- Relax and let your mind go free. It may take a while before you can release your inhibitions.

- Look inward, as you ask yourself important questions about what you want out of life.

- Do this repeatedly for short intervals of time.

- Do not expect answers all at once.

As you practice the technique of fruitful dreaming, banish anxiety and negative thoughts. There is no need now to concern yourself with the specifics of how you are going to get to that place you are imaging. In fact, such concerns are counterproductive at the start. It is important that you not be a "nay-sayer," so burdened with doubts that there is no room to soar.

When we were formulating the dream of "going for the gold," I found a photograph of the head table where the highest ranking district governors sat. One space happened to be vacant. I seized the opportunity, cut a picture of myself out of another photo and glued it onto the vacant place. During the year, when the going was rough, I'd look at that picture and remind myself of the dream. It worked. I sat in that place at the head table during the awards banquet.

> *"You see things; and you say 'Why?' But I dream things that never were; and I say 'Why not?'"*
>
> —George Bernard Shaw

Find the Time

When do you find time to visualize? You don't find time. You must take time. Few people have extra time to spend. What are you thinking about while getting dressed? Why not fast-forward and think about having reached your goals? Set aside some private time—upon awakening in the morning and just before going to sleep at night. Your subconscious is most receptive at those times when you are just becoming fully awake or just before drifting off to sleep. Our subconscious cannot tell the difference between what is real and what is vividly imagined. The key is to focus on what you want, and then vividly imagine it. Plant the seeds in the subconscious and it will work for you, whether or not you are thinking about your goal.

If you decide to pursue your dream, then you will have the power to persevere on its behalf. You will be ready to take the actions that will make it reality.

Practice Positive Affirmations

We talk to ourselves frequently, but what we usually say are put downs like, "That was stupid of me." "How can I be so disorganized?" Or worse! Over the years we have developed false humility and denied our power to influence others. We often decline to accept our own value.

Try replacing the "put downs" with positive statements about yourself and your abilities. Statements like:

> I am a unique and precious being created by God for very special purposes.

I am doing the very best I can.

I easily visualize myself having achieved all the things I now have set as goals.

I have plenty of time to do all I want to do in this life.

I am healthy and energetic.

I am ever growing in love and awareness.

My workplace is free from clutter.

My mind is clear and focused on my goals.

My life includes dear friends and loving family members.

I enjoy the love and respect of prominent people.

Thoughts flow freely from a higher power, through me, enabling me to help others lead more fulfilling lives.

I am filled with love and focused on positive feelings.

God is watching over me, protecting me from harm.

I am living the good life.

I enjoy vacations in exotic places.

I enjoy having my family around me.

How This Worked For Me

When I became single again, I was working part time. The salary was barely enough to pay the bills. One day, at work, I took out a notepad and decided to try the goal-setting technique. Looking ahead five years, I decided I wanted to be a mid-level manager. I had no idea where that thought came from, and not the slightest idea of how to bring it into reality. I wrote it down in the form of a goal.

I then began thinking about how I could possibly make it happen. I discovered a training program, which would allow a person to progress systematically from one grade to the next with experience and training. The catch was that entry was based on a test score. The possibility of getting into the program was slim. I was told there were few openings. The qualifying score was 60, so I set my sights on 65, thinking that would be competitive.

I purchased a book with practice exercises and set about cramming for the test night and day. I visualized successfully passing the test and repeated positive affirmations frequently. Though it sometimes seemed hopeless, I persisted.

The results were amazing. My score of 89 catapulted me to the top of the list and I was accepted almost immediately into the program. Within three years, I had tripled my salary. Within four years, I was a mid-level manager! I am convinced that the key was writing that goal on paper. I became focused and determined.

> ### *Claim Your Outcome*
> *Visualize the outcome you want.*
> *Vocalize your claim in the present tense,*
> *as though you already owned it.*

Chapter 21

Implement the Plan

Things don't always go according to plan. But without a plan, things could be a lot worse. Even a poor plan, enthusiastically pursued, is better than an action taken with no plan. You need to be flexible.

Having an action plan will be of great value in helping you keep focused. There will be many opportunities to deviate from your chosen path. When the road seems too difficult and you become too tired, a look at the clearly defined path of an action plan can boost your spirits. Modify the plan as you go along, taking note of things you have already accomplished.

Take the First Step

Bring it home. Nail it! This is where the rubber meets the road. Expend some energy. Try not to think of it as hard work; you may resist it. This is time to DO IT! Find something you can do today that will advance you on your journey. You don't need to know all that needs to be done to achieve what you want. However, you must be able to find something that you can do immediately to start on the path you have chosen.

> *"It's healthy for everybody to have to deal with the unexpected because it allows people to consider things they haven't considered before, to behave in ways they haven't behaved before."*
> —Constance Newman

Plan and Implement

Your determination to take action will be an early indication of the probability that you will succeed. It is easy to dally when you are breaking new ground with goals that make you stretch. Inertia is hard to overcome. The longer we look at what needs to be done, the harder it becomes to get ourselves moving. We can study a situation all day long. The key is to get into action. Once we have taken the first step, the second is easier, if taken soon afterward. "Bite the bullet" and do it. Notice the small successes along the way. It is okay to quietly pat yourself on the back.

If you delay the start of your journey, you are not truly committed and will probably not reach what you said at the beginning was your heart's desire. It would be better to stop at this point and go back to look for another dream.

Be Persistent

Take the first step, then take the next step. Look ahead and see what holes you can fill in now. Wishy-washy people want things, but they are not willing to work toward them. They are those who wish upon a star—always wishing, sometimes praying, never investing time or energy in what they say they want. Don't be an idle "wisher." Define your dream, decide to have it, then develop an "I will until..." attitude.

> *"Success is 99% failure"*
> —Soichiro Honda, Founder
> Honda Motor Corporation

"I will keep on trying, finding a way around obstacles, overcoming barriers, until I reach my objective or make a conscious decision to change direction."

Know When to Walk Away

On the other hand, at some point along the way, it may become evident that what you thought was a great idea, your vision of the future, also has insurmountable obstacles. There is no need beating yourself to death, butting your head against a brick wall, to MAKE something happen. Stop and evaluate the situation. We do not have to "win" at all costs. The best course of action, when this happens, is to pull back and clear your mind. Let go of the problem. You may find an inspirational moment when something just "happens," someone smoothes the way in front of you, and you can again move forward. Perhaps another great idea surfaces.

Life is not a straight line. There are many twists and turns and ups and downs. There are also abrupt stops and false starts. The prime objective is to take advantage of the good times, cope with the bad times, and be grateful for what you have. Pauline, a colleague of mine who is a physicist and an artist, puts it best, "Run on the downhill stretches." You will have lost nothing for having progressed in the direction of your dream. Think of all the experiences you have gained that will serve you well in everything you attempt.

How do you know when to walk away? Books can help. Study. Learn from other people's experiences and mistakes. Learn from personal experience. Accept responsibility and look for lessons in your failures. By making small decisions daily, consciously in line with your vision, and evaluating the outcome compared to the cost, you will become a better judge of what is best for you and those dear to you. Learning, changing, growing, that's what life is all about!

Develop a Sense of Urgency

Do it now! The circumstances won't improve with time; the obstacles will not evaporate. Once you develop a burning desire to have something, and you have taken the prudent steps outlined here, you are well on your way to achieving it. Review your action plan often. Formulate positive affirmations that support your efforts, visualize the outcome you want, and continue to do whatever it takes. You will achieve your dream.

Put the Plan into Action
Don't delay; take the first step.
Be persistent.
Accept change.

Chapter 22

Lessons Learned During the Burial of the Unknown Soldier

Listen, can you hear it? The faint sound of a trumpet drifting across the gently sloping hillside dotted with white crosses. The hazy mist makes it seem far away. Hear it? "Day is done–gone the sun–from the lake, from the hill..."

My first job with the Army was developing the logistics support plan for that State Funeral, the Burial of the Unknown Serviceman from Vietnam. The desired outcome: solemn and ceremonious burial executed flawlessly.

The Third Infantry, the Old Guard, planned everything from the operational perspective. Our job was supporting them, the hundreds of very important persons who attended, and to an extent, the public. Our planning included: the caisson to carry the casket, drivers for the cars for the cortege, press stands for the media at the capitol, transportation for the masses who would go to the cemetery for the interment, comfort stations along the route of the funeral procession—all depended on us. No mistakes allowed.

We identified requirements. Who needs what, where, and when? Are they entitled to it? How will we get it where it is needed on time and in sufficient quantity? We planned backward, set milestones, coordinated, and adjusted.

There seemed to be a million and one details to think about - not enough stake and platform trucks for the media stands. How to transport the caisson? Where should the transportation command post be located?

I learned that things are not always as simple as they seem. Planning is one thing; execution is another. Putting comfort stations, port-a-johns, around the District of Columbia, for instance, is no simple task!

Planning, briefing, rewriting, coordinating. Finally, 5:00 a.m. Sunday before Memorial Day, 1984, we were on the steps of the US Capitol with the commanding general, ready to rehearse. Though I was not in the military service, I felt their pride and their reverence.

The events unfolded on the national scene on schedule: the arrival of the remains at Andrews Air Force Base, lying in state in the Capitol Rotunda. The day of the burial, there was a change in plans. Has that ever happened to you? The Chairman of the Joint Chiefs of Staff decided to walk in the funeral procession. At the last minute we had to turn the lead cars about and get them away from the Capitol. Everything else went on with precision. At last, the President's speech and then the burial. It was an emotionally charged weekend.

After every major event, we prepared "After Action Reports," looking for lessons we had learned. There were things that did not go well, or were not in the plan. The lessons were recorded for future reference.

Planning and execution on this grand scale was great training for life in general: Look ahead. Plan. What is needed to reach your objective? Where is it needed and when? What can go wrong?

The execution of plans rarely goes precisely as envisioned. Flexibility is key. Contingency planning is a must. Reviewing afterward can help smooth the way ahead. Awareness is the watch word. Know what is going on and your role in it. You can stay ahead of the game, if you look ahead. Think. Plan. Act.

> *Although the remains of that serviceman have since been identified, the importance of the ceremonial burial has not diminished. It provided an opportunity to recognize the sacrifices of the thousands of U.S. citizens who had been called to arms in an unpopular military action in the Republic of Vietnam. Many of them were assailed by their countrymen when they returned to the US. Many are still missing.*

YOUR TURN—TAKE ACTION

Take Action

1. Write your vision statement.

2. List major milestones.

3. Develop an overall strategy for achieving your vision.

Plan and Implement

4. Make a list of everything you can think of that will have to be done to reach the first major milestone. (If you run out of room here, use a note pad.)

5. Sort, prioritize, then set goals you intend to reach.

6. Visualize the outcome you expect.

7. Develop positive affirmations to supplement the visualization.

There is never a better measure of what a person is than what he does when he's absolutely free to choose.

—William M Bulger

SECTION SIX

Measure Your Progress

Chapter 23

Keep Score

You don't play baseball without keeping score; you don't play golf without counting the strokes. This is the game of life. You need to keep score so you can celebrate the "wins." Chart your progress; learn from your experiences. Keeping score helps you decide how you are going to close the gaps, the distance from where you are to where you want to be.

The Human Computer

During the middle of the 20th century, Betty Love was a "computer." Betty is also a wife, mother, and grandmother, a living human being! She had a very exciting job in the high desert of Antelope Valley in California. Betty worked in the area of experimental aircraft. It was her job to take recorded results of test flights and apply calibration data to those results. In that way, the true characteristics of the flight test could become known. The corrected data that Betty came up with was plotted on curves and manipulated mathematically to evaluate the technical performance characteristics and come up with useable data. Her tools were calculators. Betty was the computer. That was her job title.

Computers and other technological advances of the information age now sort through data and help us make sense of mounds of information in seconds.

At the close of the millennium, among many advances, computers may be used to enhance the effectiveness of radiology in detecting breast cancer in mammograms.

While your plotting and tracking may never reach the level of calculation required of Betty, the computer, you do need to keep score. When you plot your progress on a chart, you can easily see where the gap is between where you are and where you projected you would be at any time. This is a much more intelligent approach to living than constantly acting and reacting without knowing the results of what you are doing. It's hard to know if you are "winning," making progress, or "losing," falling farther away from your projected goal.

Write It Down

I am often asked, when I talk about tracking the progress of personal projects, "Do we really need to write this down?" It is important to keep some record. We forget so easily. If you have written goals, it will be easy to apply them to a graph of some sort to track your progress. You might even prefer to add some comments about the progress you have made toward your intermediate goals when you record thoughts in your journal each day. Do whatever works for you.

> *"When today is gone, we can never live it again. So don't worry about what might have been or should have been. Learn from the experience of it and make tomorrow better because of it!"*
>
> –Inez Neilson Krcelic

Establish a Baseline

The baseline is where you are now, your line of scrimmage.

You have a vision.

You have developed a plan of action.

You may have people to help you achieve your desired outcome. They jumped on board when you shared your vision with them.

You know what resources you have.

You know the critical success factors, things that must occur or that you must have to succeed.

You know the first step to take.

The object is to move forward from that baseline position. If something interrupts your progress, you will need to evaluate what went wrong and perhaps make some adjustments.

Know Where the Goal Line Is

The goal line is your desired outcome. It may be the long-range, strategic vision or an intermediate goal. How will you display that in graphic or numerical form?

The goal line may change over time, just as our vision of technology has changed over time. That does not mean we can't proceed with the information we now have.

> *"Though no one can go back and make a brand new start, anyone can start from now and make a brand new ending."*
>
> — Anonymous

We have already identified major milestones and worked out a time line. So we might designate the milestones with dates along the x, or horizontal, axis of a chart and goals along the y, or vertical, axis of a chart.

It would look something like this.

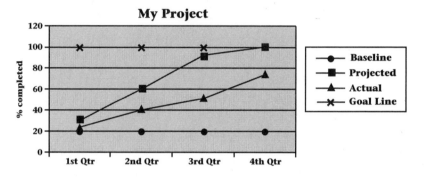

A bar chart, 3D, or area graphic may be more meaningful for what you are doing.

Find something that suits you and use it!

The object is to see how well you are progressing. With a visual display, you can see at a glance if you are on schedule, on target, and decide if adjustments need to be made. If there is absolutely no time for charting, use checklists and check off actions as they are completed. At the very least, mentally envision your progress chart.

The gap is the distance between where you are and where you projected you would be. It is usually caused when something interferes with your plans. If you find the gap getting larger, rather than smaller, take time to analyze what is happening. Focus on closing the gaps. Perhaps you need to use your available time more efficiently. Perhaps you need to reanalyze your dream and what you are doing to accomplish your goals.

Decide What Victory Is

Does "close" count? If you come close to your vision, is that success? How will you know when it is over? Are there time limitations? Must it be completed before your 30th birthday, for instance? Must you use grant money before a certain date? If we dream of living out our 50's in a house on a deserted beach, could we settle for a condominium and move on to other dreams?

Most often, there are no external finishing lines for our desired outcomes or visions. We establish them arbitrarily.

You will probably not be ready, or willing, to state such things at the outset. These considerations can be kept somewhere in the recesses of your mind and only considered from time to time.

Work with Others

If others are taking action with you as you pursue your dream, responsibilities should be assigned early on and deadlines established. You will then know where the timelines intersect. Is your action dependent upon the completion of another person's action?

Bennie Bough, co-author of *101 Ways to Improve Your Communication Skills Instantly*, and I, had independent visions. Each of us envisioned ourselves as a very successful professional speaker. The book was one item along the timeline. It was our mission for awhile.

Together, we brainstormed the contents, then went our separate ways to research and write segments. We drew up a table of responsibilities and listed all that had to be done, who was responsible for each item, and the deadline. As we brainstormed and wrote, we held informal "in-progress reviews." We wanted to be sure that everything was on schedule so there would be no slippage as we approached the end of the project. Although we were sometimes tempted to ignore a deadline, we had established a completion, "drop dead," date early in the process. Bennie's daughter was getting married, and the father of the bride had to be finished with the project at least a week before the big event. Using occasional extraordinary personal discipline, the book was completed on schedule, nine months after conception. It now has been translated into two languages. It is being published in four countries, and is in its third printing.

> ***Measure Your Progress***
> *Write it down!*
> *Establish the base line.*
> *Display the goal line.*
> *Focus on closing the gap.*

Chapter 24

Take Care of Details

State the Rules

This is your life. It is your plan. It is important that the rules allow you to win. You have your basic rule book, core values and purpose. But what are the rules for this vision? Are you going to hold out for perfection? Will you accept less?

Vicki is proud of her son who is a very intelligent and studious high school student. When he brought home a straight "A" report card, she was overjoyed and congratulated him. "It's not so good," he told her. "I only got 95 on the final English test. I should have gotten 100. I messed up."

How often do you beat yourself up because you are not perfect? Or, worse yet, degrade your children or spouse because they are not perfect? Of course, we can strive for perfection, but we must recognize our imperfections, at some level, as acceptable. Otherwise, we place enormous stress on ourselves. We need to build in checkpoints that would allow us to congratulate ourselves or others.

Conduct IPR's

Schedule some in-progress reviews or IPR's. Compare current status with the goal line and milestones. If you keep doing what you are doing, progressing at the same pace, will you hit the target? Will you arrive at the desired outcome at the time you set as your goal?

If your analysis indicates that you are going to miss the mark by a wide margin, you have certain options:

1. Continue what you are doing and hope for a miracle.

2. Reassess how you are doing things.

3. Reevaluate how much time is needed and lengthen your time line appropriately.

4. Look for more resources; hire help, if possible.

5. Expend more time and energy on task; decrease free time.

6. Lower your goal line; settle for less for now.

7. Give up. Realize this may be more than you can accomplish at this time due to circumstances beyond your control.

Provide Feedback

If there are other people helping you or even encouraging you in your quest, let them know how it's going from time to time. We are usually more inclined to share good news. It puts us in a good light. But sometimes, we see ourselves "spin-doctoring," making events seem better than they are. This is done by hiding some facts, stretching the truth, and sometimes, just plain lying. That's not necessary for you to do. You are accountable only to yourself.

When the news isn't good, face it. Maybe you did

"drop the ball," fail to follow through. Admit it. At the same time, state how you plan to correct the situation or overcome the delay. Your report might look something like this:

CURRENT STATUS:
    Two months behind projected completion date.

WHY? (Be objective, no excuses, just facts.)

    —situation beyond your control

    —situation within your control

CHANGES TO BE MADE:

NEW PROJECTED COMPLETION DATE:

When you present the unfavorable facts truthfully, with optimism, your support team will most likely cheer your honesty, integrity, and determination.

If, on the other hand, you focus on the struggles and your disappointments, you may be seen as sniveling or whining. Your team will be more likely to give up on you before you do. If you have decided to continue pursuing your dream, let them see your optimism. They are more likely to sign on for the long haul if you show your resourcefulness and maintain an "I will until....." attitude.

> *"The more faithfully you listen to the voice within you, the better you hear what is sounding outside of you."*
>   — Dag Hammarskjold

> **Check project status.**
> *Details may make the difference between success and failure.*
> *Fill in the gaps.*
> *Provide feedback to support team.*

Chapter 25

How We Kept Score

When I was serving as district governor, we needed to get information out quickly. We wanted to display it so that it took only a small amount of time to digest.

We developed a simple graphic, called our Power House, which was displayed at every opportunity. The graphic conveyed our status at a glance. There was a foundation depicting our history. The main floor consisted of our goals and accomplishments to date. Our club extension goal was the roof. Each roofing tile represented a new club. The tiles were coded to indicate the state of development. Black meant, "It's in the bag!" Stripes indicated, "It's in the works." Blank tiles indicated there was no activity.

Our goal was 35 new clubs within the year. Six months into the year, we had chartered only seven new clubs and had several more in earlier stages of development. It did not seem possible that we would reach the goal. After another month, we lowered the goal to 25 new clubs. That was still high. We felt it was within reach and still felt positive, though challenged! At the end of the year, we had chartered 24 new clubs. We missed our stated goal, but still achieved our desired outcome. Not only did we rank in the top six districts in the world, we were #1!

You can devise some way, other than the usual charts and graphs, to depict progress toward your goal. Keep it simple. Make it meaningful.

New Clubs
■ **Chartered**
≡ **In-Process**
☐ **No Action**

Projected
200 CTMs
50 ATMs
10 SC

Actual to Date (Nov)
CTMs 95
ATMs 20
SC 3

B A S E L I N E

POWER HOUSE

YOUR TURN—TAKE ACTION

Access Activity

1. How will you know when you have succeeded?

_____
_____
_____
_____
_____
_____
_____
_____
_____

2. What are the critical success factors for your dream?

_____
_____
_____
_____
_____
_____
_____
_____
_____
_____
_____
_____
_____
_____
_____
_____

3. Review your system to track your progress over time. Does it cover all facets of your life, or only your current goal?

_____
_____
_____
_____
_____
_____
_____
_____
_____
_____
_____

4. If you keep doing what you are doing, will you reach your goal? ____ yes ____ no

5. What adjustments need to be made, if any?

_____
_____
_____
_____
_____
_____
_____
_____
_____
_____

6. What have you invested in the successful outcome of your efforts in time, money, energy?

7. Does it exceed your projections?

8. How have you adjusted your plans to accommodate the difference?

9. Who is most responsible for your progress thus far?

10. How sure are you of team members' continued support? Anticipate changes.

Give me someone as I wander through life who cares about me, someone who picks me out of the crowd, notices me, remembers me, makes me believe I'm special. This is the plea churning about within every human being. It is the greatest hunger in life.
—Robert Conklin

SECTION SEVEN

Rewards

Chapter 26

Reward Efforts

More people will begin to believe you can achieve your vision when they see small signs of success. The most difficult part of your journey will be moving from inertia—getting a new project off the drawing board. That is precisely when you will find the fewest number of supporters—when you need them most. Do not be disheartened. Just buck up and take that first step, then the next, and the next. When your friends and family see your determination and the small successes you have accomplished, they will become more enthusiastic supporters.

Rewards and recognition are:

> Pleasures or treasures, something that is pleasing to the recipient
>
> A sign of another person's appreciation or esteem
>
> Symbolic repayment of a debt

There is prestige and status attached to receiving rewards and recognition.

Know When to Praise

Rewards, awards, and thanks should be given soon after earned. As soon as you enroll other people, begin to give small "rewards." A sincere "thank you" can be reward enough for small favors or assistance. Showing appreciation for another person's actions costs you nothing.

One effect of rewarding others is to encourage them to repeat the behavior you value. Find things for which to be grateful. Provide some sort of recognition. It may be just a pat on the back or a thank-you note, but the message it sends is important. It lets them know that their assistance is valued. It says you care.

A secondary effect of rewards may be that other people, who become aware that you are a person who shows appreciation, will want to assist you, too. Showing your willingness to recognize the efforts of others will draw people to you.

Give Something Appropriate

Do not overdo it with grandiose, lavish gifts. Recognition and awards should be commensurate with the activity for which they are being given. If you go to extremes, people will see that you are trying to call attention to yourself, and not just saying "thank you" to them. The spotlight should be on the recipient. You should not expect to get anything from it.

> "Glory ought to be the consequence, not the motive of our actions."
> —Pliny the Younger

Be careful not to brag, as some people take that as a challenge. At the same time, do not deny yourself the pleasure of recognizing a job well done. Review the tips on communication so you get the good news out appropriately.

Tie Rewards to Goal Getting

As a goal is reached, and at various times before it is reached, it is appropriate to recognize the efforts expended—to encourage the heart. We can't always wait to judge results. Sometimes it takes a long time to reach a goal and our spirits begin to sag. We need encouragement to stay the course. One of the people who helped me tremendously, and was always near at hand, was especially fond of chocolate covered peanuts. So there was always a bag stashed away for the special moments, either in celebration of a job well done, or a hug when times were tough. It is always appropriate to recognize efforts that lead toward the goal.

It is helpful at the outset to say, "When we reach this point, achieve this goal, we will have a certain reward." "When I've lost ten pounds, I will treat myself to a trip to New York." A reward is an enticement to persist, an additional motivation to stay the course.

> **Provide Recognition**
> *Show Appreciation.*
> *Smile and say "thank you."*

Chapter 27

Please the Recipient

Rewards mean different things to different people. "Put my name up in lights!" "Don't let anyone know about this." One person's treasure, though, may be another person's trial. In one instance, the recipient is eager for the public recognition to be gained by the presentation of the award. In other instances, due to shyness, or possibly envy and backbiting in the workplace, people want no fanfare at all. The challenge is to discover what people prefer and reward them accordingly. A married man in my office was not interested in a monetary award; he preferred to have extra time off to spend with his family. Another man, who had a large family and was the only wage earner, preferred a cash award.

Know What to Praise

Praise the behavior you want to happen more often. Need to move your team forward in the office? Think of recognizing small successes in unusual ways. Consider individual, as well as team, awards. Is a bonus in order? Tie the award to the level of effort being rewarded.

Need help with household chores to make time for your "magnificent obsession?" Would rewarding the children with money for the movies get your desired result? Perhaps the answer is rewarding yourself by hiring help for those mundane things that must be done, but which do not move you toward your goal.

Know How to Praise

Have you ever been presented with an award and felt like the presenter was insincere, or that the award was downgraded in the eyes of the audience? Do not pass on that kind of behavior. If you are going to award someone, make it meaningful. Make the recipients feel special. Let them, and any audience gathered for the occasion, know why the award or "thank you" is being given, what the award is, and if there is any special significance to the award.

Gathering informally with your support team occasionally will boost their spirits and rekindle their interest in your personal project. These can be excellent times to give public recognition to deserving individuals.

Consider lingering for an "after glow" when a significant milestone has been reached successfully. An after glow is created when key people take time to be together after others have left the site of a gathering. This is another special time to relax and savor the achievement or simply enjoy the feeling of closeness.

Give Them What They Want

The Platinum Rule, according to Tony Alessandra is "Do unto others as they would have done unto them." In other words, find out what the person who is to receive the recognition would prefer and give that to him.

> *"More than money and more than sex, people want recognition and praise."*
> —Mary Kay Ash

This is a different perspective from, "What's in it for me?" Your focus now is on what's in it for them—the people who enrolled in your vision and helped you along the way. Perhaps they saw pitfalls you didn't notice, introduced you to the broker who got you the loan you needed, held a party so you could meet more people, or typed that thesis for you.

> *Rodger Flagg, owner of EXPRESS SEARCH, INC, had a goal of increasing the size of his business by 25% in one year. He enrolled his employees and the contractors who worked with him in the Patent and Trademark Services business. Part of his persuasive technique was offering them a 10% pay increase if the vision was brought to fruition. When the group was committed to making it happen, Rodger immediately gave each the 10% raise. That way, he demonstrated his faith in his vision and his faith in the workers. That year, the business increased 29%. The following year, Rodger again believed a 25% increase was possible. He encouraged the employees to find ways to decrease expenses and make the business more profitable. Again, he paid the bonus up front and again, his team significantly surpassed the goal.*

Think of Creative Ways to Reward People

Try something out of the ordinary. One of the military men on my staff in the Pentagon wrote the book on using civilian resources to augment government personnel in the area of logistics, the Logistics Civilian Augmentation Program, or LOGCAP. Their services were critical in the 1990 conflict in the Middle East. There were not enough military and government civilians to provide all the transportation, supply, and maintenance that the uniformed forces needed. No one knew exactly what would be required, but substantial civilian support halfway around the world was an obvious need. With three days notice, our expert was to be in Saudi Arabia to set the program in motion. He was to be there 45 days; he returned almost a year later.

I wanted to recognize his contribution to that effort, and to the program as a whole. Military personnel cannot receive monetary awards. What's the next best option?

There are only two Pace awards given each year: One is given to a military person and one to a civilian. Logisticians rarely receive it. I set my eye on that prize and personally wrote the recommendation. It was a thrill to be with our soldier and his wife when the Secretary of the Army presented him the Pace award.

On one particular occasion, two of our officers did an outstanding briefing on an exceptionally difficult topic. As I sat down at the computer to send them a congratulatory E-mail, it occurred to me that others on the staff were also deserving of appreciation. As I contemplated recent events, I found that every member of the staff could be singled out for a specific achievement. The note went out to all of them, pointing out accomplishments of each, noting my appreciation, and that of our chief. Morale shot through the roof; you could feel a change in the energy level in our area. It didn't take long for the note to find its way to the

> *"He who wishes to secure the good of others
> has already secured his own."*
> —Confucius

upper echelon. That was not the intent, but it did provide added recognition for some well-deserving personnel.

Find unusual ways to single out someone and say "thank you" in a special way.

SPECIAL NOTE:

The White House Greetings Office will send greetings from the President free of charge for significant events such as: retirement, graduation, sympathy, get well, Bar Mitzvah, Bat Mitzvah, birth, Quinceanera, 50th wedding anniversary, and 80th birthdays.

Requests must be received six weeks in advance of event. Request must include the requester's name, address, and phone number, and the name and mailing address of the recipient. For birth congratulations, add date of birth. The card will be sent in the baby's name. For other significant events, include the date of the event or other specific date the greeting should be delivered. Send request to: The white House Greetings Office, OEOB Room 39, Washington, DC 20502. Requests may be faxed to: 202-395-1232. Autographed photographs of the President and the First Lady are also available upon request.

Praise Publicly
Be creative.
Be sincere.
Be timely.

Chapter 28

Reward Yourself

Plan on it. There will be plenty of reasons to reward yourself. It may be difficult, but it's essential. Sure, kudos from others are rewards, but it's also important to be good to yourself. Take some time off. Treat yourself to a weekend getaway—even if there may be a seminar along with it. Take that exotic cruise around the Greek Isles that you've dreamed about. Ski the Matterhorn, as well as the local mountains. Invite a friend to dinner. Go to a movie, the theater, or the beach. Go ahead, treat yourself!

One of my favorite treats when I lived in the Washington, DC, area, was to take the train to New York City, a four-hour ride. From the train station, a person can wander quite a distance in the city without buses or taxis. The city is noisy and invigorating. I love it! I usually attend plays or musicals or visit a museum. One special Thanksgiving Day, my daughter, Resa, joined me in New York. We shunned the Thanksgiving Day parade and headed for the Statue of Liberty and Ellis Island. We had a wonderful, unhurried time seeing the sights, while the crowds were downtown. What a luxury!

What is your favorite get-away? How do you reward yourself? Once, when I brought up this subject in a seminar, the participants were surprised at the idea. Of course, rewarding yourself can be overdone; we're not talking hedonism here! All of us need encouragement from time to time, and treating ourselves to something special is a good way to get that encouragement when it is not forthcoming otherwise.

At other times, a specific achievement calls for a reward. When a friend of mine retired, she treated her husband and herself to a trip to Paris. Look for special occasions to treat yourself.

Awards, rewards, and recognition are all very important. However, they should never overshadow the value of the activity that leads to the achievement and subsequently, the reward. It is through the activity that we learn. It is through the activity that a kindred spirit with others develops, an esprit´ de corps´. It is through the activity that people feel a sense of belonging and bonds of friendship are formed.

A ninety-year-old multimillionaire once shared with me some words of wisdom. He said that "being" a millionaire was never as much fun as "becoming" a millionaire. The thrill was in overcoming the challenges he encountered along the way. The excitement was in the risk of implementing innovative ideas. Happiness was in his interactions with people.

It is not what you get when you achieve your vision that is of utmost importance; it is what you become in the process of striving for it.

That's life! Give it all you've got!

> ***Stay the Course.***
> *Plan personal rewards.*
> *Celebrate!*

ADDITIONAL RESOURCES:
1001 Ways to Reward Employees, Bob Nelson and Ken Blanchard

Your Gold Medal Of Life!

Take charge of your life! Live it to the fullest with your eyes wide open. Be fully awake and aware. Appreciate everything that happens to you; some things will be pleasurable, others will be painful. Learn lessons from both.

Lift your sights. Look at the stars, especially when things seem darkest. Know that there is a higher power in the universe; you are not alone. Practice humility; accept help.

Take responsibility for how your life is going. You are in control through the choices you make. Don't try to dodge the consequences. If you never take the blame, you can never accept the rewards. Be willing to take calculated risks. The thrill of the game of life is charting a course, accepting problems as challenges, facing them head on, and holding someone else's hand along the way. Sometimes you win, sometimes you lose. Keep your eyes, not on individual battles, but on the outcome.

Hold onto your vision. You worked hard to form it. You deserve it. Be willing to work hard for what you want. Don't let pride overcome you. Keep your own counsel. Do not become over-awed by other people. Know your power. Use it wisely.

The past is history. The future is unknown and uncertain. Live to the fullest in the present moment. Make the most of it to achieve your vision—your Gold Medal of Life.

YOUR TURN—TAKE ACTION

Reward Efforts

1. What types of awards/praise are you prepared to give those who participate with you in "chasing your dream?"

2. Look back at Section Five and consider how you might reward yourself and others at milestones along the time line.

3. Ask others how they like to be rewarded—within reason.

4. List some of the things you can accumulate in advance for "on the spot awards," such as certificates, mugs, candy bars, etc.

5. What types of awards do you enjoy receiving?

6. What type of recognition is available to you, either for yourself or to give to others?

Selected Readings

Alessandra, Tony, Ph.D. and Michael O'Connor. *The Platinum Rule*. New York: Warner books, Inc. 1996.

Allen, James. *As A Man Thinketh*. New York: Grosset & Dunlap, 1984.

Anderson, Walter. *The Greatest Risk of All*. Boston: Houghton Mifflin Company, 1988.

Baber, Anne and Lynne Waymon. *Great Connections: Small Talk and Networking for Businesspeople*. Manassas Park, VA: Impact Publications, 1992.

Baber, Anne and Lynne Waymon. *52 Ways to Reconnect, Follow-Up and Stay in Touch*. Dubuque, IA: Kendall/Hunt, 1994.

Bristol, Claude. *The Magic of Believing*. New York: Simon and Schuster, 1992.

Buzan, Tony. The *Brain User's Guide: A Handbook for Sorting Out Your Life*. New York: E.P. Dutton, Inc., 1983.

Canfield, Jack and Mark Victor Hansen. *The Aladdin Factor*. New York: Berkley Books, 1995.

Celente, Gerald. *Trends 2000*. New York: Warner Books, 1997.

Cetron, Marvin and Owen Davies. *American Renaissance*. New York: St. Martin Press, 1989.

Chopra, Deepak, *The Seven Spiritual Laws of Success*. San Rafael, CA: Amber-Allen Pub., 1995.

Selected Readings

Collins, James C. and Jerry I. Porras, *Built to Last*. New York: HarperBusiness, 1997.

Condrill, Jo and Bennie Bough, Ph.D. *101 Ways to Improve Your Communication Skills Instantly*. Alexandria, VA: GoalMinds, 1998.

Conklin, Robert. *How to Get People to Do Things*. Chicago: Contemporary Books, Inc., 1979.

Covey, Stephen R. *The 7 Habits of Highly Effective People*. New York: Simon and Schuster, 1989.

Davidson, Jeffrey P. *The Complete Idiot's Guide to Reaching Your Goals*. New York: MacMillan, 1998.

Eskes, Dave. "No Fear of the Dark." Hope Magazine. February 1997: 46-53.

Fadiman, James. *Unlimit Your Life: Setting and Getting Goals*. Berkeley, CA: Celestial Arts, 1993.

Fitton, Robert A., Ed. *Leadership: Quotations from the Military Tradition*. Boulder, CO: Westview Press, 1990.

Frank, Milo O. *How to Get Your Point Across in 30 Seconds or Less*. New York: Simon and Schuster, 1986.

Garner, Alan. *Conversationally Speaking*. Los Angeles: Lowell House, 1997.

Gracián, Baltasar. *A Pocket Mirror for Heroes*. Ed. and translated by Christopher Mauer.. New York: Currency Doubleday, 1996.

Selected Readings

Haines, Stephen G. *Successful Strategic Planning.* Menlo Park, CA: Crisp Publications, Inc., 1995.

Helmstetter, Shad. *Choices.* New York: Simon and Schuster, Inc. Pocket Books, 1989.

Helmstetter, Shad. *What to Say When You Talk to Your Self.* Scottsdale, AZ: Grindle Press, 1986.

Hemsath, Dave and Yerkes, Leslie. *301 Ways to Have Fun at Work.* San Francisco, CA: Berrett-Koehler, 1997.

Hill, Napoleon. *Think and Grow Rich.* North Hollywood, CA: Wilshire Book Company, 1966.

Hill, Napoleon. *The Science of Personal Achievement.* (Audio Tapes) Niles, IL: Nightengale Conant., 1992.

Jingwa, Daniel. *Blue Sky Thinking.* Wilmington, NC: BR Anchor Publishing, 1998.

Johnson, Robert S. "TQM: Leadership for the Quality Transformation ." Quality Progress May 1993: 83-85.

Koberg, Don and Jim Bagnall. *The Universal Traveler.* Menlo Park, CA: Crisp Publications, Inc., 1991.

Lee, Blaine. *The Power Principle.* New York: Simon and Schuster Fireside, 1997.

Morris, Tom. True Success: *A New Philosophy of Excellence.* New York: Grossett/Putnam, 1994.

Nelson, Bob and Ken Blanchard. *1001 Ways to Reward Employees.* New York: Workman Publications, 1994.

Nierenberg, Gerard I. *The Art of Creative Thinking*. New York: Simon and Schuster, 1982.

Peale, Norman Vincent. *Positive Imaging*. New York: Ballantine Books, 1996.

Peale, Norman Vincent. *The Power of Positive Thinking*. New York: Simon and Schuster, 1994.

Phillips, Donald T. *Lincoln on Leadership: Executive Strategies for Tough Times*. New York: Warner Books, 1992.

Province, Charles M. *Patton's One-Minute Messages*. Novato, CA: Presidio Press, 1995.

Renesch, John. *Setting Goals*. San Francisco, CA: Context Publications, 1983.

Rosenberg, Marshall, Dr. *Nonviolent Communication: A Language of Compassion*. Del Mar, CA: Puddle Dancer Press, 1999.

Schwartz, David J. *The Magic of Thinking Big*. North Hollywood, CA: Wilshire Book Co., 1959.

Schwartz, Peter. *The Art of the Long View*. New York: Currency Doubleday, 1996.

Smedley, Ralph C. *Personally Speaking*. Santa Ana, CA: Toastmasters International, 1988.

Tannen, Deborah. *Talking from 9 to 5*. New York: W. Morrow, 1994.

Selected Readings

Von Oech, Roger. *A Whack on the Side of the Head: How You Can be More Creative.* New York: Warner Books, 1998.

Weiner, Valerie. *Power Communications: Positioning Yourself for High Visibility.* New York: New York University Press, 1994.

INDEX

abandon, 68
abundance, 16, 32, 37
accomplish, 22, 28, 89, 108, 112
achieve, 16, 28
achievement, 17, 60, 88, 92, 117, 37, 185, 187, 190
adjustments, 163, 164
adventure, 56, 60, 81, 88
after glow, 185
Alessandra, Tony, 185
Allen, James, 18
alliances, 85, 105
analyze, 33, 35, 40, 49, 50, 164
anchor, 29
Anderson, Walter, 68
Anonymous, 90, 119, 163
apparition, 24
approval, 93
aptitude test, 28
argument, 82
Ash, Mary Kay, 185
aspiring, 35
associates, 50, 59, 85, 106, 112
attitude, 33, 56, 67, 68, 70, 81, 106-109, 122, 147, 169
awareness, 26, 38, 143, 152

Baber, Anne, 95
Bagnall, Jim, 68
balance, 40, 133, 138
bandwagon, 86, 96
baseline, 162, 163
Beecher, John, 81
behavior, 28, 40, 182, 184, 185

belief, 24, 29, 43, 49, 51, 80, 101, 139, 140
Bible, 16, 22
birth, 26, 27, 42
Blasingame, Jim, 136
blue-sky thinking, 30, 35, 38
books, 83, 102, 148
Bough, Bennie, 4, 95, 118, 165
boundaries, 30, 32, 33
brain, 49
brainstorm, 14, 62, 112, 115, 118, 165
break bread, 81
breakthrough, 112
Browning, Robert, 66
Bryan, William Jennings, 131
Burbank, Luther, 106
Burroughs, John, 106
Bush, Barbara, 50

camaraderie, 112
career, 24, 26, 27, 37, 52, 56, 106, 130
Carlyle, Thomas, 51
Carnegie, Andrew, 105
caution, 40
certificates, 15
challenges, 27, 88, 91, 109, 121, 190, 193
chart, 26, 27, 161, 162, 164, 171, 193
checklist, 101, 164
Chiang Kai-shek, Madame, 30
Chief Executive Officer, 24
Chinese Proverb, 102

INDEX

choice, 24, 25, 26, 28, 29, 46, 49, 50, 51, 191
Chopra, Deepak, 66
circle, 53, 105
circumstances, 24, 30, 39, 51, 55, 114, 149, 168
classes, 57, 58, 70, 133, 136
co-creator, 26
college, 40, 57, 70, 133
commitment, 21, 66, 68, 75, 79
community, 85-87, 98, 101, 113, 121
compassion, 80, 87, 92
Conant, James Bryant, 57
concept, 14, 105-107, 110, 111, 119, 123
Conklin, Robert, 178
connections, 32, 70, 115
consequences, 25, 193
contingency, 61, 62, 134, 151
contribution, 27, 90, 107, 108, 122, 187
control, 32, 38, 41, 51, 55, 168, 169, 193
conversation, 81, 95, 102
conviction, 85, 89, 101
costs, 51, 58, 62, 68, 148, 182
CPA, 136
creative, 25, 32, 33, 35, 39, 50, 62
creative thinking, 39, 115
criteria, 28
cultures, 26

data, 161

death, 26, 27, 42, 148
decisions, 26, 29, 49, 52, 101, 116
degree, 40, 51, 61, 67, 132, 135, 137
Demosthenes, 67
Desiderata, 93
destiny, 131
details, 132, 141, 150, 167
determination, 21, 67, 83, 85, 96, 107, 109, 147, 169, 181
determine, 54, 115
devils advocates, 81, 97
dimension, 110, 113
discipline, 29
discretion, 135
district governor, 141, 171
diverse, 121
Donne, John, 79
downhill, 96, 148
dream catcher, 53, 54, 64, 65

Edison, Thomas A., 106
education, 28, 51, 97, 130
Einstein, Albert, 33
embarrassment, 55
Emerson, Ralph Waldo, 76, 85
empowerment, 51
endeavors, 120
energy, 28, 38, 40, 51, 56, 58, 59, 82, 85, 90, 111, 113, 121, 136, 146, 168, 187
enroll. 82, 86, 101, 110, 181
enthusiasm, 56, 81-86, 89, 96, 101, 119, 122, 136

INDEX

entices, 24
environment, 40, 133
envy, 109, 184
Erasmus, Desiderius, 133
events, 27, 28, 30, 42, 62, 132, 133, 151, 168, 187
exercise, 70
expectation, 27, 38, 40, 108, 114
expert, 187
extraordinary, 16, 22, 30, 60, 92, 109, 131, 174, 166

facets, 109, 131, 174
factors, 49, 67, 70, 131, 163, 173
failure, 67, 70, 81, 82, 131, 147-8
family, 24, 26-7, 29, 37, 39, 42, 55, 58, 61, 80, 134, 137, 143-4, 181, 184
fantasize, 139
feedback, 168
feelings, 85, 87, 101, 116, 129, 143
finish line, 25
Firestone, Harvey, 106
fixity, 57, 66, 67
Flagg, Rodger, 186
flexibility, 151
force, 24, 38, 57, 105, 110
Ford, Henry, 29, 106
formula, 107
fortune, 64, 133
Franklin, Benjamin, 28
free will, 26
free-flowing, 30

Galileo, 94
Gandhi, Indira, 38
genesis, 56
Give It All You've Got, 118, 190
Gracián, Baltasar, 80
goal line, 163, 167, 168
Goethe, 40
good will, 108
graduation, 27
Grandma's Law, 135, 136
gyroscopes, 49

hallucination, 24
harmony, 105, 107-9, 111, 116, 118
Hazlitt, William, 63
health, 37, 39, 137, 143, 146
heart, 38, 42, 63, 66, 138, 147, 183
heaven, 66
Herzl, Theodor, 66, 67
Hill, Napoleon, 105, 117, 119
Holley, Donna, 27
home, 30, 34, 39, 90, 112, 139, 146, 167
Holmes, Oliver W., 134
Honda, Soichiro, 147
honesty, 29, 169
horizon, 32, 54, 61, 62
Howe, Edgar W., 93
Hubbard, Kin, 67
Human resources, 59, 133, 134
hurdles, 51

images, 89, 139

imaginations, 25, 30, 32, 33, 35, 37, 39, 50, 85, 98, 112, 121
impact, 87, 119
impossible, 29, 33, 35, 36
in-progress reviews, 116, 167
independence, 29
infirmities, 67
influences, 28, 51
information, 61, 87, 92, 112, 116, 135, 161, 163, 171
insights, 59, 120, 122
integrity, 29, 169
Internet, 92, 134, 139
investments, 51, 61
island, 79, 82, 189

James, William, 139
Jung, Carl, 66

Kennedy, John F., 33
know how, 16, 82, 108, 168, 185
Koberg, Don, 68
Krcelic, Inez, 162

law enforcement, 56, 57
leads, 108
legacy, 27, 42, 60
Levin, Kenneth, 33
lifeline, 26-28, 42
limitations, 120, 122
Lincoln, James, 113
list, 28, 29, 52, 79, 80, 86, 132, 133-36, 144
lives, 29, 35, 46, 51, 152, 61, 109, 143

lottery, 32
loyalty, 29
luck, 50
magic, 40, 107
magnificent obsession, 184
management, 26, 61, 130, 133
master-mind, 105-07, 110-112, 116, 119, 120
masterpiece, 76
material, 25, 59, 108
MBA, 61, 132, 136, 137
McCall, Nathan, 67
membership, 97, 115, 116
memory, 42, 94
mentor, 70, 79, 80, 118, 135
merit, 96
Michelangelo, 29
Middle East, 21, 187
milestones, 37, 136, 150, 164, 167
military services, 57, 151
millennium, 161
mission, 25, 32, 33, 34, 130, 165
mistakes, 148, 150
money, 28, 51, 58, 61, 90, 106, 135, 165, 184, 185
Mother Theresa, 25
motto, 96

NASA, 33
neighborhood, 30
newsletter, 86
Newman, Constance, 146
notes, 83, 86, 94, 95, 114,

146, 155, 182, 187
notions, 32
obstacles, 29, 39, 51, 54, 56, 61, 91, 97, 98, 109, 130, 147-149
on stage, 81
opinions, 80, 101
Options, 57
orators, 67
outcome, 49, 53, 66, 68, 81, 87, 89, 91, 129, 130, 132, 137, 148, 149, 150, 163, 167, 171, 193

parameters, 29, 30, 39
parents, 27, 61, 80
partner, 34
passion, 24, 91
passionate, 40, 92
payoff, 59
Peale, Norman Vincent, 40, 41, 139, 140
Penn, William, 64
perils, 50
perks, 64
permission, 32, 97
Perry, John J., 24
persevere, 68, 82, 142
picture, 35, 37, 39, 87, 101, 109, 129, 139-141
pitfalls, 186
plans, 55, 61, 62, 89, 112. 151, 164
pleasure, 25, 181, 182
Pliny the Younger, 182
plotting, 162
poor, 25, 146

possibilities, 30, 33, 35, 50, 118, 130,
Powell, Colin, 67
power, 29, 32, 40 ,49, 50, 51, 66, 68, 81, 105, 110, 115, 116, 129. 142, 143, 193
powerful, 16, 38, 51, 57
powerlessness, 67
Power House, 171, 172
predisposition, 81
price, 23, 58, 62
pride, 151, 193
principle, 24, 106, 119
problem, 55, 56, 57, 62, 63, 119, 148, 193
process, 21, 22, 35, 37, 40, 46, 49, 53, 54, 80, 82, 85, 87, 93, 109,112, 114, 140, 166, 190
project, 21, 40, 83, 116, 162, 166, 181, 185
promotion, 27, 52
purpose, 25, 57, 66, 67, 107, 108, 113, 115, 118, 142, 167
pursue, 33, 40, 57, 68, 142, 146, 165

qualities, 39, 113

Raphael, Sally Jesse. 67
ratio, 68
reaction, 68, 89
realization, 25, 60, 108
reasons, 25, 189
Reeves, Christopher, 67
report card, 167

INDEX

Republic of Vietnam, 152
research, 34, 165
resources, 51, 54, 58, 59, 79, 90, 111, 112, 130, 163, 168, 187
responsibility, 28, 66, 113, 118, 148, 193
restrictions, 33, 35
results, 57, 67, 87, 105, 106, 108, 112, 115, 121. 122, 137, 144, 161, 162, 183, 184
reward, 60, 83, 138, 181-184, 189, 193
risk, 30, 51, 54, 55, 64, 68, 81, 90, 91
Roosevelt, Eleanor, 46
Rufus, Quintus Curtius, 88
rules, 28, 114, 167, 185

sacrifices, 61, 152
satisfaction, 25, 29, 60, 111
Saudi Arabia, 187
scenarios, 61
scholars, 35
school, 26, 39, 56, 167
Schwartz, Peter, 58
score, 144, 161, 174
scrimmage, 162
search, 80, 85, 186
security, 37, 59
self-confidence, 38, 108
Shaw, George Bernard, 141
Shirley, Pauline, 118
sidelines, 85
Sioux, 53
skills, 22, 57, 58, 63, 64, 80, 86, 92, 108, 111, 113, 116, 118, 123, 165
Smedlley, Ralph, 56
soul, 17, 129
spirit, 105, 113, 116, 190
spirits, 146, 183, 185
spiritual, 37, 110, 122, 137
stake, 16, 79, 101, 150
stand-up comic, 111, 113
stars, 37, 193
status quo, 32
stepping stone, 23, 51
stereotypes, 94
Stick-to-it-ivity, 67
strengths, 28
stress, 58, 63, 136, 167
stretch, 33, 35, 96, 120, 147
stuck, 38
subconscious mind, 49
success, 21, 25, 51, 55, 79, 81, 116, 122, 129, 131, 147, 163, 165, 181
symbols, 107, 139
synergy, 119

Tannen, Deborah, 95
target, 132, 164, 167
task, 26, 34, 40, 50, 151, 168
teacher, 30, 39
Tead, Ordway, 126
team, 86, 87, 105, 120, 169, 177, 184-186
techniques, 37, 61, 88
terminate, 116
terms, 24, 49, 51, 89
test, 28, 49, 98, 144, 161, 167

INDEX

thank you, 93, 181, 182, 185, 188
theme, 118
thoughts, 16, 25, 37-39, 41, 88, 105, 141, 143, 162
threat, 55
Toastmasters Club, 85, 92
Tomlin, Lily, 35
tool, 27, 64, 161
tracking, 162
trade off, 58
tradition, 27

universe, 40, 87, 193

values, 24, 28, 29, 43, 90, 113, 137, 167
"what if, ", 61, 62
view, 21, 26, 81, 109, 121
vision, 17, 24-26, 29, 30, 33, 37, 40, 42, 49, 51, 52, 59, 63, 66, 66, 68, 70, 79, 80, 83, 85-87, 89, 90-93, 98, 191
visualized, 68, 129, 139, 142-144, 149

Wardinski, Mike, 118
Washington, Booker T., 79
Waymon, Lynne, 95
webbing, 53, 54
Weihenmayer, Eric, 39
welfare, 30
West, Mae, 114
Williams, Bev, 112
Winkler, Henry, 89
Wishy-washy, 147

work life, 27
world view, 26
world, 24, 26, 29, 32, 40, 67, 87, 91, 126, 134, 137, 187

Zionist Congress, 66

THREE EASY WAYS TO ORDER
Call: 800-697-5680
Fax: 661-274-9015
Mail: GoalMinds®
   P.O. Box 902092
   Palmdale, CA 93590-2092
E-mail: MillePrimer@goalminds.com
www.goalminds.com

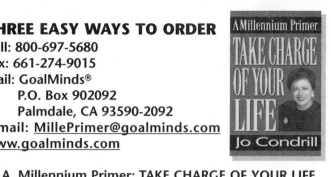

__ A Millennium Primer: TAKE CHARGE OF YOUR LIFE $21.95

__101 Ways to Improve Your Communication Skills Instantly
   audio cassettes (2) English or Spanish $19.95

__101 Ways to Improve Your Communication Skills Instantly
   128 page Book $14.95

__Empowering Communication Skills for Women (Video) $19.95
   Ground Shipping   3.00
   CA Residents add 8.25% State Sales Tax
                                          Total $_____

For information on Jo's business services: Coaching, and Consulting; Seminars, Speeches, Workshops and 3-day Retreats, Please call 800-697-5680, or E-mail MillePrimer@goalminds.com

Name_____

Organization_____

Address_____

City/State/Zip_____

Tel_____E-mail_____

Payment:

( ) Check Payable to GoalMinds®
( ) VISA ( ) Master Card ( ) American Express ( ) Discover Card

Card No_____

Name on Card_____Exp Date_____

Signature_____
   Required for credit card purchases

**GoalMInds® • P.O. Box 902092 • Palmdale, CA 93590-2092
800-697-5680 • Fax: 661-274-9015**